W9-BOM-904

No Ordinary Life
Memoir of a WWII Bombardier

Sue Johnpeter

Copyright © 2014 Sue Johnpeter
All rights reserved

Cover design by Bill Wylie, Wylie Design

ISBN: 1499146833
ISBN-13: 978-1499146837

In memory of my beautiful Dottie

G.K.

In memory of my father, Frank Littell

S.J.

Photo of B-17 *Aluminum Overcast* by Jeff Lautenberger

The bombardier's view.

INTRODUCTION

I first learned about Glenn King during a church sermon. Our minister spoke of faith, hope and a tuna can, all carefully tended by a twenty-one-year-old bombardier captured by the Germans during the last months of World War II. Glenn's story – of how a Red Cross can of tuna became a talisman against despair and fearsome hunger – captivated my attention. Here was a story that needed a wider audience – and a book deal.

Finding Glenn after the church service, I urged him to write a memoir. But as with many great storytellers, he was more comfortable telling his history, not writing it. For years, he had honed his tales about flying and surviving in front of hundreds of middle-school students in Naperville, Illinois.

Gradually, as he started to consider the idea of a written record, we sat down together in his home in the Fall of 2013. This tall former roughneck from Wyoming began to tell me about his life. "What it amounted to," Glenn's charming way of introducing a story, began the tale of what happened on March 2, 1945, when Harold S. Davidow missed the briefing and 2nd Lt. King took his place on a B-17 Flying Fortress headed into Germany.

It was Glenn's twenty-third combat mission. And his last.

Sue Johnpeter
Naperville, Illinois

CHAPTER ONE

MIDWEST, WYOMING

Like a lot of ten-year-olds, Glenn King was crazy for airplanes. By 1934, he was a card-carrying *silver* member of the Junior Birdmen (you had to be sixteen to be ranked gold). He was also in good standing with the Roscoe Turner Flying Corps, Roscoe being a famous aviator and barnstormer from the First World War.

Eighty years later, Glenn still has those membership cards, paper-clipped to the black pages of a scrapbook meticulously kept by his mother, Alice, in their home in Midwest, Wyoming. By the time Glenn was twenty-one, the scrapbook was filled with scores of news stories cut from the Casper *Star-Tribune* about the pounding the 8th Air Force was giving Germany from its bases in England. After the war, Glenn would annotate those news accounts with his mission numbers, giving his parents a clear and terrifying confirmation of what their bombardier son and his crew had been doing from October 14, 1944, until March 2, 1945.

But in 1934, it was enough to dream about flying a plane over the Salt Creek oil field where he lived. The Midwest Oil Company (eventually Standard Oil, and Glenn's future employer) had profitably drilled this part of Natrona County since 1921, though oil had been extracted from the earth long before that. In fact, oil bubbled so readily to the surface of the earth that pioneers a century earlier had stopped here to oil their wagon wheels. Or so the story went.

The entire town – grocery store, barber shop, library, Post Office – was owned by the company. By 1921, Midwest and the satellite town of Edgerton had a combined population of 10,000 people, with more arriving every day. Among them were Leslie King and his brothers-in-law, Emil Friedholm and Bill Easton.

A mechanic whose hands were as comfortable with a coping saw and lathe as they were with a torque wrench and a welding torch, Leslie knew hard work. He'd been providing food for his family and working the family farm since the age of fourteen when his father died.

Leaving young wife Alice Friedholm and baby Glenn on the family farmstead ninety miles east of Bismarck, Leslie struck out for the oil fields in 1924 in search of a job and good wages.

Given the scope of the oil field, which was producing thirty thousand barrels a day, there were jobs aplenty. In short order, Leslie was employed and living in company housing. In time, Alice and Glenn would be reunited with their husband and father six hundred miles from home.

"I was raised on the basis, 'Be a good boy, or your Dad will get fired,'" Glenn recalled. "My Dad's boss lived right across the street." And while that served to keep Glenn on his toes, Leslie ultimately would become the boss, and the pressure would let up.

The Kings moved to Lewis Street, where Glenn bought a black and white terrier pup, named Jack, who was so devoted to his young master that he burned his paws by constantly running after his bicycle. So, using half of a small wagon, Glenn built a trailer and attached it to his bike. With a few pieces of wood railing added for safety, the world's first canine mobile device was born.

"He loved riding in that thing," Glenn recalls with a laugh, confessing that once in a while, he would yield to his lesser angels and ride through a mud hole "and splatter him good." In short order, Jack learned to peek around the bike, turning his head at just the right moment to avoid a mud bath.

With his dog in tow and buddy Charles Townsend from across the street as his wingman, Glenn spent his youth flying through Midwest. He loved to watch his father fix cars, learning enough so that he, too, would one day be able to do whatever was required to maintain them. That apprenticeship would serve Glenn very well. Knowing how things work, or can be made to work, would shape his future as a bombardier and as an engineer.

Summer's bike rides gave way to more serious pursuits, such as employment and getting in shape for sports. During high school, Glenn worked in the service station for two years on weekends and in the summer. (And for those unfamiliar with what a *service* station did back then, Glenn would like you to know that it was gas pumped for you, a chamois carefully run across the windshield, checking the oil *always*, and gauging tire pressure. For free.)

The station's owners, "real good people," lived right on the property. "I'd close and take the cash box to them when the station closed, and then babysit their son. That was for a dollar a day, plus tip, in 1940. The next year I got the biggest raise I ever got, percentage-wise – to two dollars a day!"

While the ten-hour days were manageable, opportunity knocked hard when Fred Goodstein offered Glenn fifty cents an hour (seventy-five cents on weekends) to dig up old buried pipelines for scrap. Goodstein, an entrepreneur who would go on to make a fortune in the oil business, was then running a brisk business, selling scrap metal to the Japanese.

"Digging ditch," as Glenn calls it, was pretty good work and meant a veritable fortune for someone "just trying to have enough money to buy a hamburger for my girlfriend, Fran, and five gallons of gas instead of three.

"After the second day, my muscles were sore. I found out I could get a pretty good rest if I went to get a drink out of the watering can." Goodstein's agent, a real SOB in Glenn's recollection, observed Glenn and yelled, "Hey you! We don't pay you to drink water. Get back in the damn ditch!"

3

Yes, sir.

"The last day I worked, when a flatbed trailer came to haul away what we'd dug up, he chose me to throw the iron on it because I was taller than everyone else. He also told me I was eighteen, not seventeen years old." Adding a year meant keeping things on the up and up.

While Glenn was happy to keep mum and have the extra money, realizing later that the Japanese sent back that metal in the form of bullets has given him pause over the years.

When Glenn went out for high school football in 1938, he was six-foot-one and weighed one-hundred thirty-five pounds. The following year, he'd grown an inch and weighed one-hundred eighty pounds. While he was trying to coordinate all of that newly acquired physique, he was put on the "scrub team."

Midwest was scheduled to play Douglas High, but given the distance, the teams would meet up on a field in Casper. And, of course, the band would be there too, a conundrum for Glenn. He played first trumpet in the band, "so shortly before, as the bandmaster was making the arrangements, the principal, Miss Lucille Niles, told those of us in the band, 'I've talked to coach. For those of you, like Glenn, on the scrub team, you go ahead and suit up in your band uniform and perform the first half. After, you can suit up for the game during the second half.' Boy, I was steamed. I went up to her and said, 'You made a deal with coach and I can't do anything about that. I'm going to go ahead and be in the damn band for the first half and suit up for the second half, but that's the last time I ever toot this damn thing.' And it was. I was really upset. It was humiliating."

Miss Niles, who would one day marry Bandmaster McKenna, was among the many teachers to call on the Kings after Glenn was shot down over Germany. She would tell his parents and brother Jerry that she was completely confident that Glenn would be okay and survive the war. He's never forgotten that kindness, though if he had his druthers, he'd be happy to forget the game.

On Feb. 24, 1942, just as World War II was revving up, Glenn celebrated his eighteenth birthday with a first-ever friends party. "My parents knew what was coming, relative to the war," so every stop was pulled to stage a candlelit dinner with Glenn's favorite – chicken and home-made noodle casserole, followed by his Mother's renown thirteen egg-white angel food cake.

A miniature tomahawk, hand carved from wood by Mr. King, marked each place setting with the guests' names: *Glenn and Frances. Bob and Pearl. Timer and Charlotte. Frankie and Gerry.* A much larger hatchet with everyone's names carved on the "blade" accompanied the cake. Glenn has treasured and displayed these keepsakes through the intervening years.

"Dad knew his way around a coping saw," Glenn says, showing other glories his father crafted from wood: a miniature hammer made from a ball bearing with a handle whittled from a Model T spoke, a carved wood scimitar and miniature wood pliers that actually open and close. These exquisite pieces of art have been carefully preserved by Glenn. They evoke his father and the admiration he has always felt for him.

"My Dad could do anything," he says.

Leslie King was particularly adept in knowing a boy's heart's desire. "My parents gave me a 1930 Plymouth the day I came home with my report card from Eighth Grade, in 1938. My grandmother told me that my parents had gone to the town of Edgerton on an errand, so I was to stay at home. When they came back, Dad was driving my little Plymouth, with Mom following in our car."

Glenn knew all about servicing a car, right down to painting his own whitewalls with rubberized paint. If there was something he didn't know how to do, his Dad showed him. It was up to Glenn to do the work, except on one notable occasion.

"On Christmas Day in 1940, I had been out that night with the car and came home late. The next day, it was real cold, below zero for sure. I started it up and it quit working with a colossal BANG. Instead of buying oil for it, I had been using free used oil from the filling station that I worked in, because the car used a *lot* of oil." The water in the used oil had accumulated in the engine, got to the oil pump and "tore hell out of the engine. I sat through the rest of Christmas vacation without my car.

"Afterward, my Dad tore the engine down, saw what was damaged, went to the wrecking yard in Casper, got the pieces, put it together and rebuilt it. That really speaks for my Dad," Glenn says, clearing his throat.

But before the newly acquired parts could be fitted in, a remnant of the broken camshaft would not budge. Mr. King tried any combination of fixes without success, until it dawned on him that an electromagnet would do the trick. So he built one, a solution devised by a man who had grown up with kerosene lamps in North Dakota and had taught himself the principles of electricity via a correspondence course.

The old part was extracted, its replacement installed and Glenn drove his beloved first car until 1942, when he sold it before leaving for the University of Wyoming. Glenn had added in a rumble seat to accommodate more riders. His brother, Jerry, twelve years younger, occasionally would hide in the covered seat in the fervent hope that he could jump out and scare the living daylights out of his big brother. (This never happened.)

Glenn was one of only three Midwest High School kids who actually owned a car. Best pal Bobby Cooke had a 1929 DeSoto. Glenn and Bobby managed to cook up a little fun on the outskirts of Midwest: As their cars approached from opposite directions, there being minimal road traffic in those days, "we'd immediately recognize each other. We had it rigged up if we had anyone with us, before we passed each other, we'd swoop a little as a signal. That meant as we got to each other, we'd swap lanes as we went by." The infamous lane switch, designed to make the passenger's hair stand on end and/or heart stop, occurred between Midwest and Edgerton. "It said a lot to how close we were, and how confident we were in each other." Glenn adds it also speaks to "how stupid you can be in high school."

When it came time for graduation, there had to be *something* to commemorate such a milestone. What with the freedom that comes to those who own a car and the siren call of Casper, Glenn and Fran, Bobby and Jackie, and Bob and Pearl, piled into Bobby's 1934 Chevy after the last dance. (Bobby had upgraded his ride from the DeSoto, thanks to a profitable paper route.) They arrived in fine style about 1 or 2 a.m. "Everything was closed up!" Glenn says.

Whether anyone had thought of this possibility before leaving Midwest goes unremembered. In any event, that was beside the point, which was to do *something*, and all three couples had.

"On our way home, it was about daylight, and we began to wonder if maybe the sheep herder outside of town might fix us some bacon and eggs," Glenn says. "We drove out through the prairies to where he was living." Apparently the breakfast request was met with a few choice words, and the six graduates turned around right fast and scooted for home.

Glenn had done well in school. He had played football as a starter (defense and offense) and basketball (poorly, in his recollection). His girlfriend Fran gave him a pen and pencil set for graduation that he would carry with him throughout the war. His car was featured in *Black Gold*, Midwest High School's yearbook. His eye was now set on an engineering degree, probably in aeronautics, at the University of Wyoming at Laramie.

Glenn and classmate Eddie Shyne made plans to room together at school, so that September 1942, Mrs. Shyne and Mrs. King drove their graduates to the Casper bus station. The boys said their farewells and rode off to Laramie. Although granted admission based on a phone call, neither boy had visited the campus. On leaving the bus station, they had to ask a passerby, "Which way is the University of Wyoming?"

That day, they found the Student Union and a map of the campus. They ran into a group of guys looking for roommates and solved where to bunk. The more pressing issue of board was worked out when they called on a boardinghouse cook in need of dishwashers. The set-up was as perfect as it was spontaneous. They then returned to the bus station to manhandle their trunks to their new home.

"This is where we grew up in a hurry," Glenn remembers. "Our parents had no idea how much things cost. We didn't know how to go to college, and our parents didn't know how to go to college."

By the end of the first quarter, Eddie would decide to leave school and join the Navy. Glenn thought he would have more time to study. Uncle Sam had other ideas.

CHAPTER TWO

TO BE A FLYER

In 1942, the last thing Glenn and every other eighteen-year-old American male expected was to be drafted. When President Franklin D. Roosevelt and Congress lowered the draft age from twenty-one to eighteen that November, Glenn received his orders to report to the draft board for a physical in December.

Meanwhile, recruiters from United States Army Air Forces were active on campus. Flying always had captured the fancy of this faithful member of the Roscoe Turner Flying Club. Not only was flying novel, it was a little heart-stopping and most definitely glamorous. Glenn's hero, Charles Lindbergh, had flown the *Spirit of St. Louis* on a solo, non-stop flight across the Atlantic when Glenn was five years old. Aeronautical engineering was his major at the University of Wyoming. It would seem the flying stars had been aligning for some time.

On the morning of December 10, Glenn phoned the draft board to ask to postpone his physical until the afternoon, to which they agreed. He had already undergone the mental and physical tests administered by the Air Corps[1] and was sworn into the service that afternoon. While

---

1 The U.S. Army Air Corps has undergone a number of name changes through the decades. When Glenn was in college, it was the United States Army Air Forces. Everyone called it the Air Corps. Ultimately, Glenn would fly with what was and is known as the 8th Air Force.

fully expecting to take advantage of the college deferment offered by the Air Corps, Glenn was called to active duty February 25, 1943.

Glenn left the University of Wyoming with academic credit for one quarter and a smidgen of another. And while an education of a different sort would continue throughout the war, it wouldn't be until 1946 that he was able to return to a campus out of uniform.

He went home to Midwest to "play around" a bit before his folks drove him to the Casper bus station in order to fly out of Denver. The Air Corps assigned him to Jefferson Barracks in St. Louis for basic training. Fit from working in the oil fields a mile above sea level, Glenn and his fellow recruits from out West could not understand why the drill sergeant was trying to "kill them" by continuously running them up and down hills. It was late winter and cold. The cadets wore heavy wool enlisted men's overcoats and overshoes. It finally dawned on them that the ceaseless torture was because they were in excellent physical shape and never out of breath. "As soon as we figured that out, we learned to pant," Glenn recalls with a laugh.

As candidates for commissioned officers, two years of college qualified one as a cadet. Even though his academic life had been interrupted by war, Glenn's background and potential got the attention of his superiors. "The Air Force needed personnel to fly all of these B-17s, so they sent me back to college."

At the University of Missouri-Columbia, two hours west of St. Louis, Glenn and his fellow cadets lived in fraternity houses vacated for the cause. They marched in formation to and from their classes. ("I took one of the finest physics courses I ever had," Glenn notes.) And they managed to rustle up a little bit of romance by serenading the sororities whose houses were nearby.

In the basement of the house they lived in, Glenn and Wyoming pal George Kelly received permission to clean up a small room with a window as a study retreat from the crush of cadets.

One day the squadron had been restricted to barracks for rolling empty Coke bottles down the stairs. Instead of "blowing beer foam" at The Shack, Mizzou's famous watering hole across campus, Glenn and George were confined to quarters. The punishment gave them the opportunity to observe a pair of very famous legs just outside the basement window. Playwright Moss Hart, on campus to gather material for a play entitled *Winged Victory*,[2] had stopped to listen as the cadets serenaded the sorority next door. Glenn and George listened to the singing echoing back and forth while observing Hart, at least from the waist down, just outside the window.

It would be his closest brush with stardom until 1992, when Glenn and his Cadillac played extras in the movie *While You Were Sleeping* with Sandra Bullock. (Glenn says he was paid seventy-five dollars for a day's work. The car got ninety.)

After several months of condensed and intense learning, the Air Corps "figured they had stuffed us with what they wanted us to know and sent us to San Antonio for classification: pilot, navigator, or bombardier." It was November 1943.

"We were scared to death of washing out because we wanted to be flyers," Glenn recalls. And what did it take to be a flyer? "Physical ability, coordination, mathematical ability, good eyesight, and a level of stupidity," he says. "I wanted to be a pilot, but if I showed more aptitude to be a navigator or bombardier, that's what I wanted to do."

After ten hours of Piper Cub training at the University of Missouri, he realized he was "most happy when I was up there looking around at things rather than flying the darned plane. So, out of that, they classified me as a bombardier." Of course, what the Air Force wanted of you trumped personal preference, Glenn says with a laugh.

So it was off to Ellington Field, Texas, for more pre-flight training, including being subjected to a pressure chamber to see if these newly minted flyers were able to withstand the rigors of flying. In an airtight

---

2 *Winged Victory*, a play about three Americans who join the Army Air Forces to become pilots, was a popular bit of propaganda produced by the U.S. Army Air Forces in 1943 that was eventually made into a movie.

compartment and wearing oxygen masks, the cadets were treated to what it felt like to be in an airplane at 5,000 feet. In a letter to his parents and brother Jerry, Glenn wrote:

> Some of the fellows dropped out again today, but I was O.K. so I stayed. We then started up again and climbed very fast 'till we reached 10,000 feet. This is the altitude the army requires that oxygen be used, but they told us not to turn on the oxygen as they wanted us to find out what anoxia, or lack of oxygen, was like. We then climbed up to 18,000 feet and stayed there for some time. I noticed my fingernails were turning blue, but I felt fine. . . . .
>
> They got up to about 22,000 feet and things were getting pretty dim for me and I got very dizzy, so I put the mask on and I never smelled so much good air in my life.

One cadet made the mistake of drinking a bottle of soda before getting into the chamber and "climbing" to 38,000 feet. "He was in misery," Glenn wrote his family.

Some of the men had nitrogen build up in their joints, causing a painful condition called the bends. Others had the very fillings in their teeth ejected because of the intensity of the pressure. Glenn asked his folks to convey his deep appreciation to his dentist, Dr. Shidler, for the work he had done on his teeth. "For all the cavities I have had filled and all of them perfect, I think he did a wonderful job."

The test ultimately proved Glenn to be an "unlimited flyer," with no altitude restrictions.

When Glenn and his fellow cadets weren't having their physical and mental capabilities stretched to the limit at Ellington, they were being served up an oversized helping of Army folderol. "They were nasty. The lieutenant would come through and announce to the cadets that we were going to have a GI party tonight. 'Let's clean this damn place up!' So we'd wash windows, scrub floors with lye and water, and make every bed perfectly. Then he'd come in at eight o'clock and give us an inspection. 'This place is filthy! Do it again!' The grumbling occurred, but everyone became smart enough not to talk back."

In February 1944, the bombardiers were sent to training at Childress, Texas, to refine their instruction, particularly on the Norden Bombsight, an innovation in the military arsenal that would profoundly change the outcome of the war.

The bombsight enabled accurate bombing from high altitudes, but multiple factors had to be considered in its operation – the plane being pounded by flak fired from enemy guns, bomb type, winds, temperature, and drift, to name a few. The bombs were released electrically by the bombsight based on the data the bombardier was constantly entering into it. In a twelve-plane formation, or squadron, usually only the lead and deputy lead had the Norden. The other planes dropped their bombs when the lead planes dropped theirs. A combat bombardier's job was intense and complicated.

Glenn eventually qualified as a bombardier/navigator on a Boeing 17, the Flying Fortress. "The training we got at Childress qualified us to be both, except we didn't receive training in celestial navigation," Glenn explains. On a B-25, one person performed the role of both bombardier and navigator.

A bombardier-in-training was obvious from the black ring around his eye, Glenn says with a laugh. The bombsight, with its built-in telescope, had a black rubber gasket through which he viewed the target. The rubber rubbed off around his eye. "It was kind of a badge," he says.

When Glenn was at Childress, the Norden bombsight was so secret, it was stored in vaults. "As officers we were issued .45 pistols with the idea of protecting it and ourselves. We learned that if you take the darned pistols with you on a mission, when you came back down from where it was so cold, the moisture would condense on them and they would start to rust. No one wanted to sit around and clean one of those things, so we quit taking them with us."

For a pilot, "as soon as they think you can fly the darned plane, they turn you loose. Ditto the bombardier, and you'd go up and you'd have a certain number of practice bombs to drop in order to qualify." Practice bomb runs meant dropping a 125-pound bomb (usually filled with sand) on a target marked in powdered chalk. When it hit the ground, a puff of smoke and a flare would be captured by a camera in the nose of the AT-11 twin engine trainer. Accuracy was measured and the average was tallied.

During practice navigational hops, each mission carried an estimated time of arrival, which was communicated to the pilot. One day, Glenn's ETA had come and gone. "I finally said to the pilot, 'Do you know where you are?' He didn't, so he started buzzing water towers to (read) where we were." Glenn had overshot the target and the crew was flying over Kansas. They quickly established their position and were able to fly back to Childress. Radar had yet to be fully integrated into the B-17 fighting arsenal, so getting lost was an expected component of navigation training.

Despite a few detours along the way, Glenn completed his training as a bombardier/navigator. On April 29, 1944, he was commissioned a 2nd lieutenant and received his wings.

Had he chosen to be a bombardier instructor, he could have remained stateside for the duration of the war. Glenn says he was "too much of a show-off" to stay behind in a classroom. Besides, a ten-day leave was offered. He wanted to go home and see his family.

His mother insisted on a trip to Casper to have his picture taken wearing his uniform, gold bars, bombardier wings and jaunty cap, called a Bancroft Flighter. The drug store window in Midwest was crammed with dozens of 8x10 pictures of local boys who had joined the military. Glenn's picture would be added to the ranks. Most of the guys had signed up for the Navy, the ocean a compelling attraction to the boys from the arid Great Plains.

"Out of this community of six thousand people, everyone, and I mean everyone, went into the service," Glenn explains. "What has bothered me a lot is that three of my best friends didn't come back." Charles Townsend, Bobby Cooke, and Eddie Shyne would be among the nearly four hundred thousand American casualties of World War II.

When Glenn graduated from Childress, he was selected to go to radar school in Boca Raton, Florida, which used the millionaires' yacht club, the Boca Raton Club, for barracks. Because classes didn't start for two weeks, "there was nothing to do but play, so play we did," Glenn chuckles.

With $150 pay in his pocket, Glenn and a pal from Seattle, Mac McGee, pooled their resources and headed to Miami. In order to save money, they took a bus from Boca Raton to Fort Lauderdale, where they rented "the spiffiest little all-black Ford convertible you ever saw. Real white sidewall tires, too." With the top down, they sailed into Miami.

"Now McGee was quite a thinker," Glenn recalls. "He said, 'What we've got to do is cruise around,' so we started cruising the streets of Miami. And we see these well-dressed girls ogling a jewelry store." Glenn urged McGee to pull over and start the introductions, but McGee felt it necessary to air out that convertible a few more times before stopping to meet those girls who turned out to be secretaries on vacation from Michigan.

The foursome spent the entire evening in nightclubs, dancing and enjoying cocktails, which were served after-hours in teacups. "We just partied all night and dropped the girls off where they were staying. We couldn't go get breakfast until we got our deposit back for the car. We'd run out of money."

Looking back on the evening, Glenn muses, "We knew where we were going. It was a fun time with a couple of nice girls. I gave one of them my address." She ended up writing Glenn's parents to ask why he hadn't answered her letters.

The Boca life came to an end after two weeks because the Air Corps was running out of flight crews. "So they scrubbed the radar instruction and put me on a crew I ended up training with at Tampa, Florida." The war was going full tilt. Every crew was needed to bomb Germany.

That training phase, called transition, taught crews to work together as a team. Acting in concordance was the difference between surviving a mission and becoming a statistic.

The head pilot was Robert H. Starkel from Hartford, Connecticut; the co-pilot was Henry "Hank" Zmudka, from Chicago; the navigator was Robert G. Poage, from Tampa. And while there would be a few crew change-ups in the missions ahead, Glenn would mostly fly combat missions with these officers assembled in Tampa.

Because he didn't have much to do during navigational "hops," Glenn was designated personnel and weather officer for the crew. (No pay increase came with the added duty, he notes.) During training that summer of 1944, thunderstorms were plentiful and dangerous. Because Glenn had the best view of the storm clusters through the Plexiglas nose of the B-17, he would tell Starkel to turn left twenty degrees to avoid one storm, then later change the heading by ten degrees, depending on the cluster's position.

In the midst of one of these storms, the radio compass quit working. "Every time we'd go over an airbase and its beacon, the pilot would tell Poage, the navigator, 'Mark that one, we might have to come back.' So the navigator was busy marking them on the map, which was great, as long as he knew precisely where we were located" (and Glenn hadn't zigzagged the plane too much).

The radio compass, had it not quit working earlier in the night, might have helped the crew in its navigation. After hours avoiding storms and trying to find their way back to the base, they were thoroughly lost.

"We four officers talked about the whole thing. We've *got* to be down in the peninsula of Florida. Let's go ahead and take a heading due west and when we hit the Gulf, we'll be able to use pilotage (maps and visual clues) to find our way south to the base at Tampa."

The enlisted men could only wait and listen to the chatter of the pilots, navigator and bombardier.

"So we flew, and we flew, and we flew. Finally, the weather broke to the extent the radio compass was working again. We were in the northern panhandle of Florida. The first body of water we would have seen (if there had been enough fuel) would have been the Pacific Ocean."

Starkel's crew had been buzzing Georgia much of the night. Some seven hours later, and literally flying on fumes, they hightailed it back to the base at Tampa. "We were so late getting back from our mission," Glenn explains, "they had already alerted crews to look for the wreckage

TO BE A FLYER

of our plane. They didn't think we were going to make it, we'd been gone so long."

Glenn observes, "That was the last time that happened to us. It taught us a lot…. Don't let your mind be muddled with what you think is the problem, figure it out and solve the problem."

But that was not always easy, particularly when it came to Starkel, who made it harder for Glenn to do his job with the Norden Bombsight. (During a combat mission, the pilot is supposed to switch to autopilot so the bombardier can fly the plane on the bomb run, making course corrections as needed using the now-engaged Norden bombsight. It is designed so the bombardier is in total control of the plane during the time he is preparing for bombs away.)

Starkel, evidently, was not a fan of the autopilot protocol. "I had trouble with him not using the automatic pilot to my best advantage. I was upset because I was not doing well," Glenn recalls.

Détente of a sort eventually was reached, and the crew continued to fly out their differences until August 1944. It was time to leave Tampa by train and for Savannah, Georgia. Having bumped heads with Starkel in flight, Glenn would find the train ride a bit rumbly as well.

"We were picking up a plane and flying it to England," Glenn explains. "Everyone armed themselves carefully with booze. Whiskey, to be exact. Seagram's VO was about as good as you could get your hands on. So, we were on a Pullman train with the enlisted men. We were probably in one area as officers, the sergeants in another. They had their booze and were partying before going to 'the bad place.' We officers were doing the same thing.

"Well, it was about midnight-ish and the sergeants ran out of booze. Earlier, they had invited us to have a drink with them. Knowing that we had drunk some of their whiskey, when they ran out, they asked, 'Lieutenant, got any booze?'" Glenn shared what he had.

"Starkel discovered that and got all upset with me. 'We may have to get on an airplane tomorrow morning and you're helping everyone get soused!'

"I said, 'You know, we helped drink their whiskey. They ran out, and they come to me knowing I've got whiskey and I say no? No way I'm going to do that.'

"It got to the point he was pretty fired up. He played semipro football, and was a very good athlete. But I told him, 'I'm going to be fair with the guys we're flying with. We *don't* have to fly tomorrow, and I need to request to get off your crew.'"

Starkel eventually backed down, the whiskey was shared and the train pulled into Savannah.

Glenn says that when they were on the ground, "our crew always showed complete respect. They'd salute you, address you as lieutenant, but when we got in the air, it was 'Hey Glenn.' That was our crew. I have to believe it was like that on all the crews. We were a team and everybody felt a closeness." It might take a little longer to get the Old Man, as some of the crew referred to Starkel, to warm up. (The pilot was four years older than Glenn.)

Glenn and the crew were assigned to a B-17 carrying two spare engines, spare parts and possibly mail in the bomb bay. Their mission was to hopscotch the plane from Savannah to England. The crew's ultimate destination was Great Ashfield Airbase in Suffolk England, about twelve miles east of Bury St Edmonds.

Delaying their departure from the United States, however, was the weather. At least initially. Bangor, Maine, their first stop from Savannah, was offering twenty-five cent ham and cheese sandwiches and whiskey sours in the officers' club.

"We liked it so well in Bangor that the day we were briefed to fly, our radio operator started sneezing and we said, 'You've got a cold; you go on sick call!' We waited until he got released. It gave us a few more days of those delicious ham and cheese sandwiches and whiskey sours."

When the crew finally left Bangor, they flew to Goose Bay, Labrador, then over Greenland, headed toward Reykjavik, Iceland, in filthy weather. "We were flying at night, and everyone was getting sleepy. I glanced over at the airspeed, which should have been around 150. It was down to 135 or so. I called Starkel and said, 'What the hell's happening to the air speed?'"

The pilot reacted sharply and increased the rpms of the engine to throw off the ice that had accumulated on the propellers. About the same time he turned on the landing lights, which penetrated only twenty feet. "We were in a blinding snowstorm," Glenn recalls.

By the time they landed in Iceland in heavy winds, the crew was grounded. Unfortunately, there wasn't a chance to check out the officers' club menu. "Once you get clearance to take off, you have to be ready to take off." So everyone "slept" in the plane overnight, listening to the wind howl and the unheated plane shake. The next morning, they were able to take off, and very quickly, because the winds, though high, were sustained. In fact, Glenn later learned, the Starkel crew was the last to leave Iceland for some time.

Eventually they made it to England and, at last, to the final home for the B-17. That was the last he'd see of the plane they had flown safely across the Atlantic.

The men took a troop train to Great Ashfield Airbase, home to the Eighth Air Force 385th Bombardment Group (Heavy). The Starkel crew would be part of the 550th Squadron, one of four squadrons comprising the 385th.

This was hands down the farthest Glenn had ever been from home. He wondered what the base would be like, what would they do for fun and, most importantly, "I wondered what the hell it's going to be like flying in combat."

CHAPTER THREE
BOMBS AWAY

In a matter of days, Glenn flew his first mission to Cologne, Germany, with a crew piloted not by Starkel, but John W. Hyatt. Putting new flyers with experienced ones was part of combat continuing education.

The only thing Glenn remembers of that first mission on Oct. 14, 1944, is "I didn't crater. I was able to handle it."

He returned to Cologne the next day, again with the Hyatt crew, to bomb what were known as marshalling yards, or railway depots, in order to slow the transportation of German troops and supplies.

Meanwhile, back in Midwest, Mrs. King was combing the newspapers for news of her son and the 8th Air Force out of England to Germany. She clipped news stories from the Casper *Tribune-Herald* about the bombing raids and carefully tucked them into the scrapbook she was keeping for Glenn. When he returned after the war, he would read those newspaper stories about his missions and number the accounts according to the order in which he flew them:

- **Weather Grounds Heavies After Saturday Blow at Oil** (11 Nov. 1944 Coblenz: Mission # 5)
- **1200 Heavies Aid Doughboys** (16 Nov. 1944 ground support, north of Eschweiler: Mission # 6)
- **Luftwaffe Up, 8th Fighters KO 110 More** (26 Nov. 1944 Hamm: Mission #7)

- **98 Nazi Planes Bagged by 8**[th] (27 Nov. 1944 Bingen: Mission #8)
- **30 Fighters Also Lost in Big Oil Blow** (30 Nov. 1944 Meresburg: Mission #9)
- **650 Heavies Pound Reich** (15 Dec. 1944 Hanover: Mission #10)

These headlines brought Glenn's perilous life directly into the Kings' living room. The stories are heart-rending reading, even all these decades later. Some he still cannot bring himself to read.

Between the freezing temperatures, deafening noise and the fear, missions were taking their toll on the men who flew them. Sometimes, "cratering" was a slow, inexorable process. This was the case for a navigator two missions shy of a complete tour of thirty-five. In order to get him home conventionally, "They would only fly him infrequently and try to get him to settle down and get his feet on the ground, between missions." The alternative was to have him declared mentally unfit.

Glenn sat in close quarters with this man, who spent the mission "just standing up and walking all over the nose" of the plane when they flew through sky filled with flak, the deadly shrapnel that explodes from shells fired from antiaircraft guns on the ground.

As the navigator continued to walk erratically around in the plane, Glenn used his throat microphone to holler, "What the hell you doing?"

The navigator replied, "I'm a moving target. They're not going to get me this time."

It was a scene worthy of author Joseph Heller, except, as Glenn points out, while dancing around the plane, the man was not doing his job.

Glenn never flew with him again.

Another memorable near-miss for Glenn would follow in quick order.

Glenn describes his toughest mission on Nov. 30, 1944, to a synthetic oil refinery in Merseburg. There was a deadly carpet of flak generated by five-hundred antiaircraft guns in Berlin. As the squadron neared Meresburg and turned toward the target at the Initial Point (IP), there were another five-hundred guns firing on them.

"In that roughly 40 miles (to the target), I saw three of our planes go down in front of me. I was peering out, looking for parachutes. I didn't see any." He wondered if the crews had made a delayed jump, which would mean parachutes would not be immediately visible.

After bombs away, Glenn's plane got separated from the group and "we were off flying practically by ourselves. Every so often there would be a cluster of flak come up right off our wingtip. All I could think about was the Germans are going to send some fighter aircraft up to get us and this was their way of keeping us away from the bomber stream, by shooting right off our wing tips. But we were able to join the group and get back to England."

The crew had survived the deadly skies over Germany in part due to steel plates added to the B-17s for added protection and to deflect the worst of the flak. The plane had not gone unscathed, however. "There was one flak burst that jarred me as I was sitting on the seat. I couldn't see any damage to the plane, but when we got on the ground, the crew chief went to inspect it.

"He found a hunk of steel three inches long that sheared off one of the supports for the chair I was sitting in. It was lodged in some electrical components near the navigator.

"Had we been flying a foot lower, I would have had it. When they dug it out, I was out of the plane. I'm not exaggerating: My knees shook, it was that close." The shard of steel became the property of the ground crewman who extracted it. Glenn says he was welcome to the deadly souvenir.

Glenn later learned that Jack Chidley of Casper, Wyoming, who went into the service with Glenn, was shot down during that same mission and picked up by the Germans. He would spend the rest of the war in Stalag Luft 1, a prisoner of war camp of mostly flyers near Barth, Germany.

Astonishingly, the Air Force's solution to post-mission stress was to allocate two ounces of whiskey to each crew member after the debriefing. "There were some fellas who didn't like to drink, like our navigator,"

Glenn recalls. "I don't know if it was for a religious reason, but as a consequence, Hank, the copilot, and I, one of us got his. Now you've got four ounces. Then we'd line up somebody else who didn't want theirs. Routinely, we ended up with a half glass of whiskey. You'd down it rapidly and then go eat." Wartime cocktail hour was swift, but it helped settle a nerve or two.

Most missions were flown at 28,000 feet, where the outside temperature is 60 to 70 degrees below zero. The heaters on the uninsulated planes put out little heat. Sheepskin jackets, pants and boots worn at the beginning of the war had been replaced with heated flight suits. Not all the suits were created equal.

"The first mission I flew, the heated suit I had wasn't like the rest of the guys'," Glenn explains. "Theirs was a dark green, jacket-type, and pants with suspenders. Mine was like a pair of pajamas, with a big zipper on it. It was blue and looked old. I'm sure it was the first suit they used when they quit using sheepskin coats and pants."

As long as the gloves and boots stayed attached to the suit, they maintained the heat. A rheostat made it possible for the wearer to crank up the temperature to fight the cold at higher altitudes. If a flyer didn't have to move around too much, he could stay relatively warm, though frequently, boots and gloves disconnected, making for even more misery on the mission.

"One day, when I went to get my heated suit, they gave me one of the new ones, and it fit beautifully. When I came back the next time, they tried to get me to use one of the blue ones again. I told the quartermaster that I refuse to fly if I can't have a heated suit that fits me. I'd had enough of cold feet. Along this line, we understood that we could refuse to fly any time we wanted to. They never told us what we'd be doing after we made that decision, but it was well-known: You did not have to fly. So when I told this guy that if he couldn't get me a suit that fit, that got his attention. From then on when I walked in for my flight suit, they'd say, 'Lieutenant, we have yours over here in a special corner.'" It was draped on a hanger, suspended by itself in all its green and connected glory.

During another mission, the regular tail gunner was out sick, "so we had to fly a guy we didn't know." As personnel officer, Glenn was calling for oxygen checks, a protocol used as a roll call of the other nine men to safeguard against anoxia. These checks always started with the tail gunner and moved forward through the body of the plane.

On this day, however, Glenn couldn't get this tail gunner to respond. "I wasn't worried about him dying yet, but we were going up to where he could, so I kept calling him and calling him.

"I finally asked the waist gunner, 'Do you see him moving around?' The word was he looked all right. 'Can you possibly throw something at him and get his attention?' Well, we never got it. I don't know if he was faking he couldn't hear or what, but whatever it was, he never responded. I flew that whole mission wondering if the tail gunner was there or not.

"When we got back, I said, 'You'll never fly with us again.'"

On yet another mission, one of the enlisted men couldn't locate his parachute and panicked. "I was talking with him on the intercom, telling him that we've got that big green duffle bag up in the waist area of the plane and there's an extra parachute or two in there. Well, he said he couldn't find it. I finally had to send a sergeant to find it and put it on the guy."

Because his fear had overcome reason, "all he could see was bad." As for Glenn, "I was confident that I knew my job." As long as everyone else remembered theirs, they might just survive the war.

Combat missions had a routine all their own, starting with wake-up in the middle of the night, one or two o'clock. "First thing we'd do is eat breakfast. Normally, we ate a lot of green scrambled eggs (that's the way they came), but on the day we had a mission, the cook was standing there giving them to you sunny side up or any way you wanted them. We liked it, but we thought, 'How come we only get this on the day we have a dang mission?'"

25

Then it was off to briefing, a room with a screen covering a huge map of Germany. The screen was there for security as well as morale. "They wanted our attention, instead of our saying, 'Oh, hell!' when we walked in. They didn't want us kibitzing. They wanted us to be concentrating."

The officers – pilots, navigators and bombardiers – would synchronize their watches, called hacking, and break separately from the enlisted men for briefings. "From there, we would go and get our parachutes and our flying suits, and our duffle bag. In the plane, there was always an extra bag that had extra parachutes in it. The reason for that was one of our fears was that flak (shrapnel that could pierce the airplane) would go through the silk of our parachutes and melt it," rendering it useless.

"Then they would load us in small trucks and take us out to our airplanes."

After a preflight check, the men who flew the front of the plane – two pilots, the navigator, bombardier and engineer –would enter the plane via the small hatch at the left front of the plane. That is how these crew members always entered the plane. *Always.* "You reached up and curled your hands onto a piece of wood fitted in the interior, threw your feet through the hole and hoisted yourself onto the sidewalk of the plane. You'd do that every time to avoid going through that back door, because if you went through the back door, you wouldn't make it back from the mission. Everyone knew that was bad luck." The remaining four crew members, all gunners, entered the plane via the back door.

The bombardier sat on what is known as the chin turret, fitted with a chair, two 50-caliber machine guns operated via remote control, and the Norden Bombsight, which sat behind a bubble of Plexiglas. Glenn's view out the nose was panoramic.

As for the guns, Glenn would only test-fire his guns during the course of the war. "Nobody ever came at me. We did not have fighter opposition, or much of it," he says.

How a B-17 delivered its bombs was a ballet of timing, skill and favorable weather.

"As you approach your target," Glenn explains, "you put the information into the bombsight relative to altitude, temperature and the kind of bombs you're dropping. As you approach the target, you hit the IP, which is the last turn you make of the aircraft, and you open the bomb bay doors. From then on, every effort is made to fly as straight as possible and as horizontal as possible. If you end up and hit your target with a bomb sight, you will have ended up with the cross hairs right on the target. They're not moving and are just locked on there."

Then it's bombs away – to ball bearing plants, synthetic oil factories, anything connected to Germany's war machine. To Glenn's way of thinking, his war was a "sanitary" war, one fought five miles above the earth. The precision of the bombsight and the continuous battering by Allied bombers changed the tide of the war.

"We were bombing as a squadron with a lead crew that had been slowed down so they would accumulate their missions more slowly. The Air Force wanted to keep them around because they wanted experienced lead crews on the missions. Also, when they weren't flying, they were practicing, honing their skills to be as perfect as possible. It was an honor to be in a lead crew. You only had to fly 30 missions as a lead. The rest had to fly 35.

"Leads ended up flying the best planes with the top people who have additional training dropping practice bombs in England. They ended up being that good. Also they had enhanced skills and radar equipment at the tail end of the war."

Glenn says his group bombardier told him he wanted to make Glenn a lead, "but said he didn't discover me soon enough. He told me I had too many missions already to end up flying 30 as a total, so he made me a deputy-lead bombardier."

If anything happened to the lead crew and it was unable to reach the target, the deputy lead took over. "And that happened to me later on. We took over and I led them from the formation. It ended up we got separated from the main group on a turn; their targets were all cloud-covered but then they dropped their bombs. We weren't on the target, but I went ahead and dropped mine. I got a commendation on the bulletin board back at the base: *Lt. King hits a target of opportunity*." He says it was a nice piece of luck.

It would take a few more missions into the war before Glenn would fly with the Starkel crew regularly. However, the crew's copilot, Hank Zmudka, and Glenn were best pals from the get-go. "When we had free time, we'd go rent a car to go someplace. I would always have to rent it because Hank didn't know how to drive." The man who could fly a B-17 with the most skill in the tightest formation did not have a driver's license.

"Hank wasn't smooth on takeoffs and landings because he had inadequate practice," Glenn says. (As soon as Glenn recounted this story, an ear-splitting thunderclap sounded a dramatic coda to the retelling. Hank approving the tale, perhaps.)

Glenn flew deputy lead with an exceptional pilot named Charles W. "Mac" McCauley, a farm boy from Kansas, who managed to bring home his plane more than once with devastating damage.

Halfway through Glenn's missions, a mid-air collision sawed off the nose of Mac's plane. "The bombardier panicked and went immediately to the escape hatch and bailed out. The navigator didn't, but he was hanging on for dear life, with the nose gone and the escape hatch open and a 150 mph wind going through there.... Mac ended up bringing that aircraft home."

Bombardier-less, Mac's crew was "given" Lt. King as a temporary replacement. Upon hearing the news, Glenn wondered, "What kind of idiot would bring that thing home rather than bail out or land it in France? So I went to Mac. I vividly remember when I got him cornered. I said, 'Mac, I want to talk to you about when you had your crash. When you got the nose sawed off, what were you thinking that caused you to bring that plane home?'

"'Well, Glenn,'" he drawled in reply. "'I looked out to the left and there was a wing. I looked out to the right and there was another wing. I thought, 'If this damn thing's still got wings, it'll fly.'

"I ended up flying with him. And I think he was the best pilot I ever flew with," Glenn says.

Missions were rarely uneventful. Landing, take-off, mid-air collisions, fog, bombing runs, flak. The hazards were constant and, too often, daily.

"We had about a three-inch snowfall while we were gone (on a combat mission)," Glenn recounts. "As the first of our planes that landed at Bury St Edmonds came back, the landing gear buckled and they bellied in right where the two runways crossed. That meant no more planes could land. So they diverted us to another field. As they were landing their guys, a plane came in on the main runway and *its* landing gear buckled. That shut off the long runway; all we had left was the short runway. Our hydraulics were shot out so we didn't have any brakes. We came in, landed and came to the end of the runway and kept going. We were out in this plowed field headed toward the big forest of trees at the edge of the field. I'm in the process of leaving my seat because I don't want to be the first one to hit the trees.

"Mac apparently hit more power on one side and hit the rudder at same time, and literally turned that plane, and we crow-hopped through that plowed field and stopped before we got to the trees.

"I kidded him later, 'Did you practice that?'

"So now he's got to taxi out of the plowed field. We didn't want to get our boots muddied, so he taxied and got back on the runway. With the snow on the runway and no brakes, he was fishtailing, so he said, 'Hey guys, why don't you all get in the tail and put some weight on this thing and maybe I'll be able to taxi.' He did, and it helped. . . . He was just that good."

As the war progressed, it was not unknown for the Germans to resurrect a B-17 that had crash-landed and slip behind the tail of a squadron headed back to England. Prior to that bit of intelligence, the crew would congregate in the center of the airplane for landings and take-offs, Glenn says, because that was the safest place to be if the plane crashed.

"Once the Germans started tagging on and shooting down our planes, they ordered us to stay in combat positions until we landed. That's why I was still in the nose when we ended up in that plowed field."

Glenn observes that the beauty of the B-17 was "it could get you home. The B-24 could out-distance the B-17, but when the plane had problems and started losing pieces," the Flying Fortress was the surer bet. Additionally, using flak maps to avoid the worst of the antiaircraft guns, the B-17 could go up to 28,000 to 30,000 feet. The B-24 could only fly at 24,000 feet and caught the worst of it.

December 1944 marked the beginning of the Battle of the Bulge, the largest and bloodiest ground battle of the war. Weather was hideous on the ground and in the air. "The fog was so dense in England, we couldn't get off the ground," Glenn remembers. With the Germans on a massive offensive campaign in the European theater, "Our need was to get over there and knock out the marshaling yards. They'd brief us for a mission, but the fog was so bad, we'd be grounded."

Fog also made the return to the airfield perilous. Radar might indicate they were over Great Ashfield, but they literally couldn't see it for the soup. So Glenn, in the role of weatherman, sat in the nose as the crew flew 100 to 200 feet above England, calling out when trees and church steeples loomed in their path so the pilot could fly his crew home.

"One time, the fog was so bad on the base," Glenn recalls, "the wing commander was desperate. He called down and instructed two B-17s to taxi side by side on the runway in order to try to disperse the fog with the propellers. It wasn't too long before our guys called back the big dog and said, 'Sir, we now have two B-17s lost in the fog.' And no one would go near them because of the propellers."

Christmas 1944 would be remembered for its foul weather, the Allied battle raging in the Ardennes and Glenn receiving the Air Medal "*for meritorious achievement in participating in bombing attacks upon German war plants and Nazi military defense installation and communication lines in support of Allie armies in Western Europe.*" The Casper

Tribune-Herald ran the announcement with the dateline "An Eighth Air Force Bomber Station, England."

Seventy years later, the son of Mr. and Mrs. Leslie A. King of Midwest, Wyoming, says, "It didn't mean a lot because everyone was getting them."

Glenn was just shy of his twenty-first birthday. Two more clusters would be added to the medal, signifying his flying combat in twelve more missions.

Sometimes planes didn't make it back to Great Ashfield, and flyers made wardrobe provisions for that. First, it was important to make sure you were either wearing or packing your "snappy" clothes, to wit: the A2 leather "bomber" jackets, Bancroft Flighter caps and nice-looking leather boots. "We always wore enough uniform under the heated suit so that if we had to land in France, and if we were close enough to Paris while they figured out how to get us home, we would be dressed to party."

Once the crew did have a forced, temporary landing in France, Glenn recalls. "At this time, Patton was beginning to roll into France. We were occasionally given free rein. If you couldn't get to your target, but you saw a target of opportunity, you could bomb it. But with our forces crossing the Rhine River into Germany, under no circumstances were we to bomb a bridge unless it was a designated target.

"On this mission to Duisberg, I saw in front of me a bridge on the left and one on the right. As we hit the IP, I could see the lead bombardier was headed for the wrong bridge. I called the pilot and said, 'He's headed for the wrong damn bridge!'"

Because any radio communication at this point might have been from the enemy, nothing could be done to change the lead plane's direction. (By the time you're on the bomb run, a mid-course correction of that magnitude is not an option.) Sure enough, the lead plane bombed the wrong bridge. "Made a good hit, at any rate," Glenn remembers.

On the return home, their planes were in bad enough shape from antiaircraft fire that they were forced to land somewhere in France.

(For the record, there was no party, Glenn says, and about all he remembers is the food was terrible.)

"Before we got the clearance to take off and go back home, I told the pilot what I thought, and the pilot told the lead bombardier: 'King thinks we got the wrong bridge.'

"He came up to me and said, 'I hear you think I got the wrong bridge.' And I said, 'You sure as hell did.' Well, there was no confirmation of this until the strike photos in England were developed. By the time I got into the debriefing (the first plane airborne took the strike film to be processed), the group bombardier had the lead bombardier in the corner, giving him hell. Patton needed those bridges to advance into Germany."

The Americans had built a huge airstrip right next to the English Channel to land airplanes that were limping back from bombing runs. "It was their first chance to land after crossing water, and it was so long and wide, it didn't make any difference what angle you came in on, you could land. And that was its purpose.

"On this mission, which I was not on, my crew ran out of gasoline just as they were going to land. The engines quit. The pilot rang the bell, which signals 'Bail out!' so the ball turret gunner bailed out and ended up in some trees. From then on, all we ever called him was Treetop Evans," Glenn recalls with a laugh.

As they tried to come in for a landing, the flight engineer worked furiously to get the engines to catch, which they finally did. Starkel landed the plane. (One presumes Treetop Evans didn't have too far to walk to catch up with the crew.)

The flight engineer was highly skilled with the mechanics of the airplane, especially the temperamental bomb bay doors. "Sometimes we couldn't get them closed. That uses extra fuel to fly with those things open. He'd have to put on portable oxygen and a mask and crank the doors manually." Glenn asks, "Who's doing the flight engineer's job if he's having to fix the damn bomb bay door?"

On one mission, "the pilot literally 'dumped' the airplane to avoid a mid-air collision," Glenn recalls. "That caused the bombs to break and float. Some broke loose from their shackles, fell and hit the bomb bay doors. The doors opened and some of them fell out. The radio operator (Clayton Land) and I had the privilege of going back and sorting out what was left.

"What it amounted to," Glenn says in his homespun way of explanation, is "those bombs literally crashed on those doors and forced them open, and messed up the mechanism to close them. We had to fly back home with the bomb bay doors open.

"When we landed and taxied into our revêtement, all of a sudden this guy comes screaming in – a lieutenant, captain, I don't remember. 'Where's the bombardier? Where's the bombardier?' He was shouting, 'Why in hell didn't you shut the bomb bay doors?'

"I was in no mood to be criticized. I unloaded on him, rank be damned. I told him we had to dump the airplane, the bombs fell through those damn doors, and there was no way I could get them closed. He backed off and was gone."

While Glenn couldn't do anything about the weather, he could do something about the electric motor powering the bomb bay doors, which frequently froze up after flying thirty to forty miles after the IP in sub-zero temperatures. "When you turned away from the target, you'd want to close them right away. It was a serious problem." And while they didn't freeze open every time, it was a worry and took the engineer away from his mechanical duties and right to the hand crank.

Recognizing that the bombsight came equipped with a heated jacket that was never used (the Norden worked as it should in all weather), "It suddenly dawned on me if we could get some of these bombsight heaters wrapped around those damn bomb bay door motors, maybe we could close the things."

Glenn headed to the group bombardier and recommended the jackets be modified to fit around the door motors.

"He thought it was a brilliant idea, so they went ahead and rigged it up. They came and got me and said, 'Since you came up with this silly idea, why don't you go with us and we'll test it.' So we flew around for a couple of hours at 32,000 feet. That was as high as I'd been on any mission, and it took us forever to get up there."

When they finally achieved altitude, Glenn clicked the toggle to open the doors, flew for a long time in the minus sixty degree temperatures, then clicked it closed, a test he repeated over and over during the next few hours.

The electric jacket worked like a charm.

Glenn explains, "Until the day I was shot down, I lost more friends in mid-air collisions than to enemy action. A lot of that was inexperience of new pilots, I think. The other was, you put a thousand planes in the air and there are the vapor trails that come with those. You're flying in formation, as close together as you can. You can be flying along, you can't see and suddenly you're in clouds. The procedure is to kick rudder and slide away from each other. But for the neophyte, when all of a sudden he's flying formation, too close for comfort, the normal reaction is to pull back on the stick. And that cuts the plane above him in two. . . . And that's what happened to many of those guys."

To this day, Glenn has two small black and white photographs tucked under the glass of his oak desk. One is a shot of him standing with his pals from the Armbruster crew. "We were real close with these guys."

Exactly one day before Glenn would be forced to bail out over Germany, Charles J. Armbruster and his crew were flying over Ostend, Belgium, when another B-17 in the formation collided with them. All save two were lost. Glenn describes it with difficulty.

"They were climbing to bombing altitude over Ostend and encountered cloudy conditions. The tail was sheared off. The tail gunner couldn't get out, so he just sat there and had time to light up a cigarette on the way down," Glenn learned from the tactical officer after the war. (According to the 385th Bomb Group Association history, tail gunner Joe Jones descended 12,000 feet in a piece of the aircraft tail. The slow descent of the light-weight tail created if not a feather-light landing, at least a non-fatal one. A Belgian farmer cut him from the wreckage and took him to a field hospital, where he was treated for minor injuries.)

"The navigator on that crew, Howard Tripp, was a Californian. He was a good party boy and just a real cut-up. You could plan on it that he would come back from the officers club just about the time they closed, or a little later.

"Our barracks were very cold. We had little potbelly stoves to keep warm. The fuel we used were the cardboard rings that housed the bombs as they were transported to our planes.

"The rest of us were trying to sleep, and ol' Tripp would be telling stories and then he'd announce, 'It's cold in here! Let's warm it up a bit!' He'd get the crash axe and start hacking away at those rings. This was expected, almost every night," Glenn laughs.

"He was a case. I liked him a *lot*."

In the other photograph on his desk, Glenn and his pals – Hank Zmudka, Bob Poage, Tripp, Starkel, Armbruster – are posing with Glenn in a bomb shelter on the base, having first lined up their liquor bottles. The shadow of the photographer is cast on to the dirt wall. Glenn doesn't recall who took the picture.

So young, all in peril.

As the war ground on, building up terrible losses, the Air Corps started spreading out the missions to give crews a bit of relief from the relentless days of flying combat.

The 385th Bomb Group at Great Ashfield, comprised of the 548th, 549th, 550th and 551st squadrons, hosted dances on the base, and if there was one thing 2nd Lt. King loved to do, it was dance.

Back in Midwest, when he was a high school freshman, "take-charge Baptists from the South" moved into town, he recalls. The kids would get together and have fun on Saturday nights. "That was fine by me, but it wasn't too long before we were asked to sign a pledge card to not dance." Some of his pals signed, but not Glenn. "That's when I dropped out of the group." Good thing, too. Not only would he meet his future wife, Dottie, on a Denver ballroom floor, but on the occasion of the 385th's 200th mission, the Glenn Miller Orchestra (without the band leader) played at Great Ashfield. Glenn remembers Col. Jimmy Doolittle flew in for the soirée, too. (Doolittle led a squadron of B-25s on a retaliatory raid on Japan in 1942, for which he received the Medal of Honor.)

Girls from Ipswich and Bury St Edmunds also attended Saturday night dances on the base, mainly for the food that was served, Glenn says. England had been at war since 1939. Everything was scarce, especially food. Dance partners in uniform and midnight snacks concocted from canned corned beef meant everyone could put the horrors of war on hold, at least for a night. While the countryside where the base was located was, for the most part, spared the ravages of war, Glenn and the B-17 crews frequently saw German V-2 rocket bombs launched from Holland hurtling toward London as the Americans flew in the opposite direction toward Germany.

Obtaining leave and getting off base also went a long way toward temporarily forgetting the war. Glenn and Hank Zmudka took a train up to Edinburgh, Scotland, in search of a little fun. "We got there, and things looked dead, so we jumped on a train to Glasgow to see what it looked like," Glenn recalls. "The Navy had gotten there just before us. There were sailors all over, so we climbed back on the train and went back to Edinburgh."

The real fun, however, was in London, some seventy miles from the Ipswich train station. A photograph of Glenn standing in Trafalgar Square with pals Bob and Hank captures one visit. Standing with arms loosely draped over each other's shoulders, they flank one of the four enormous bronze lions that guard Nelson's Column, the memorial to Admiral Horatio Nelson, naval hero of the Battle of Trafalgar.

On one of those excursions, Glenn met "a real sharp gal who worked for the Bank of England. Her claim to fame was, every time I would go and see her and go to a dance, she would always have a bottle of VAT 69 Scotch."

They had fun together at the dances, Glenn says, but as far as his dance partner was concerned, after March 2, 1945, Glenn never showed up again. And she probably never knew what happened to him.

CHAPTER FOUR

ATTACK! ATTACK!

The clerk in charge of recording the Operational Missions of 2nd Lt. Glenn W. King must have used his thumbs to type. After Jan. 28, 1945, he recorded only targets – generally misspelled – and forgot to include the dates on which the missions were flown. Glenn has kept this paper record all these years. Thanks to the 385th Bomb Group Association's online database, a few of the blanks can be filled.

To get a sense of the relentless schedule of a B-17 crew in combat, Glenn's missions are listed here. Italicized words are corrections to the original record.

1. 14 Oct. '44 Cologne
2. 15 Oct. '44 Cologne
3. 22 Oct. '44 Hamburg
4. 30 Oct. '44 Recalled
5. 11 Nov. '44 Coblenz
6. 16 Nov. '44 ground support
7. 25 Nov. '44 Hamm
8. 27 Nov. '44 Bingen
9. 30 Nov. '44 Leitz-Merseburg (*Leipzig*-Merseburg)
10. 15 Dec. '44 Hanover
11. 28 Dec. '44 Coblenz

12. 30 Dec. '44 Mannheim
13. 13 Jan. '45 Mainz M/Y
14. 20 Jan. '45 Heilbrown (*Heilbronn*)
15. 28 Jan. '45 Duisburg
16. *(9 Feb. '44)* Dulmen
17. *(date unknown)* Dresden
18. *(16 Feb. '45)* Wesel
19. *(21 Feb. '45)* Nuremburg (*Nuremberg*)
20. *(date unknown)* Berlin
21. *(28 Feb. '45)* Kassel
22. *(1 March '45)* Ulena (*Leuna*)
23. *(2 March '45)* Dresden (MIA)

Glenn had just flown back-to-back missions to Kassel and Leuna. He was exhausted. It was also payday. Surely the crew would get some time off, maybe even enough leave to head down to London with Hank. But on this cold March 2, 1945, he and the crew were in their accustomed battle stations on a B-17, engines warming and on standby. If a bomber were to abort, Glenn's crew would be expected to take that slot.

When they got word they would not be flying, "There was a big hoo-ray," Glenn recalls. Sleep was at hand. Plus he owed a guy some money and now he could pay him back.

Glenn was gathering his canvas duffle out of the nose hatch when a jeep came screaming up, the driver yelling, "Where's Lt. King?"

A crew completely unknown to Glenn was one bombardier short and minutes from take-off. "I was really unhappy about having to fly that day," Glenn recalls with a glint in his eye. "I'd never heard of the crew, didn't know anything about them." Even worse – much worse – Glenn had to get on the plane via the back door rather than the nose hatch because the whirling propellers made access too dangerous.

While not entering the plane via the sacrosanct hatch was the second strike, the first was in the form of Harold S. Davidow, the bombardier assigned to the mission. He was a no-show at the morning's briefing.

Whether he was AWOL, hungover or asleep on his cot in the barracks never has been determined.

(A check of the 385th BGA database does show that Davidow was bombardier on successive missions through March and April 1945. Glenn's only contact with him would be through a post-war dream, in which he walks through the waist of a B-17, sees a man he presumes to be Davidow, grabs him by the collar and beats his face to a pulp.)

Entering the plane via that unlucky door, the only time he ever did, "I was mad the whole damn day. As I went through there, I don't think I said a word to any of the enlisted men, I was so ticked off. And when I got to where the pilot and copilot were, I said, 'Here's your goddamn bombardier.'"

The pilot, Kenneth Tipton, had flown twice in combat, the day before and once the previous week. March 2 would be his crew's first combat mission.

In the company of approximately 409 planes, Tipton flew his furious bombardier and crew toward Dresden's marshalling yards because the Ruhland oil refinery, their original primary target, was covered by clouds. For the record, Tipton's plane was in the tail position, the most vulnerable place in the formation. In the briefing, crews had been told that the winds aloft were forecasted to be so intense, their return speed to base would be 95 mph, rather than the usual 150 mph, making them easy pickings for the enemy.

Because of their inexperience, combat protocol had yet to be worked out by this rookie crew. "When we were flying combat, I trained my crew so that if we were hit by fighters, we would call out where they were coming from in a way that's clear and easily heard," Glenn says. "For example: 'Fighters coming in at 6 o'clock level.' Every bit of that is very easy to hear and understand.

"As we were flying along, all of a sudden I started seeing some flak here and there. On the intercom, I heard a little panic in voices saying what sounded like 'Flak! Flak!'

"These neophytes," Glenn recalls thinking. "Their first mission and the flak is really upsetting them."

But what they were yelling was "Attack! Attack!"

"Horrible procedure," Glenn says.

American P-51 Mustangs, which had been protecting the formation like "bees around a hive," left the periphery to engage the enemy.

In an instant, Glenn's plane was rocked hard by what he believes were the 20mm cannons of a Focke-Wulf 190. There wasn't much time in that moment to discern the ordnance caliber because both left engines were on fire.

The nose of the plane bubble, inches from Glenn's face, was massively pockmarked with holes, and the front of the plane was a snowstorm of pulverized Plexiglas.

Tipton broke out of formation.

"When we were hit, it destroyed the ailerons in the wings," Glenn explains. "The plane dipped left, and both pilots were pressing on the rudders with all their force, trying to put it into a turn, or keep it from going into a dive."

Tipton had followed protocol and set-up the autopilot before going into combat, Glenn explains. When the plane started to dive, the autopilot was activated in one quick motion, preventing the plane from spiraling. It is impossible to bail out of a spinning airplane because centrifugal force pins you to the interior of the aircraft. Under the pilots' guidance, the plane eventually righted itself, well away from the formation. Procedure had saved their bacon, but only so far.

"I called the pilot, and said, 'Number One and Two engines are on fire!' At that point, I don't think he even knew it. Bear in mind, what I thought of this crew and because I knew nothing about them, I had no confidence."

As Tipton and co-pilot Ed Craig fought to keep the plane from spinning out, Glenn radioed again to say he would salvo, or dump, the bombs. He kept a watchful eye on the engines.

"When I saw the fire, I knew we were in big trouble. How long can that fire burn before the wing breaks off or the plane explodes?" Glenn wondered.

Fire extinguishers proved useless.

Only a few minutes had passed since Tipton's plane had been attacked. The plane was now flying at an approximate altitude of 12,000 feet.

When Glenn saw molten metal blowing off the engines' cowlings, "that was the clue to get the hell out." He radioed the pilot and said, "I don't know how long you're going to stay with this thing, but your bombardier is leaving now."

The pilot typically is the one to give the order to bail out and sound the alarm. Glenn never heard it.

Glenn relates how barracks talk among the officers probably did more to prepare him for what would happen next and in the following three months than anything he had learned in a classroom. What-if scenarios were hashed out all the time. For instance, if you bail, do you make a delayed jump, where the body is in free fall? It's less dangerous because you're going to put a lot of distance between you and an exploding plane in a hurry. You can only live about two minutes at that altitude, but two minutes will get you to where there's adequate oxygen. And it was known that German fighter pilots would shoot at soldiers fluttering down in their parachutes. So, yes, maybe best to delay jump.

And if you get caught? Chuck the bombardier wings as fast and far away as possible. No telling what damage Allied bombers may have wreaked on your captors' loved ones. Best to be the navigator. That's safer and, for Glenn, the truth.

As for the life insurance papers you filled out before leaving on your first mission, you name your Dad as the contact person because you know your Mom won't be able to take it if something happens to you. That makes the most sense of all.

Glenn got up out of his seat, passed the navigator and made his way to the nose hatch. "I grabbed the emergency handle and kicked out the door, which was sucked out into the slipstream."

The next step was another what-if that had been talked about around the base.

"We were supposed to roll into a ball so you didn't hit your head on the ball turret. I don't think the guy who told us this had ever practiced this, especially with a big parachute clipped to his chest." It also seems unlikely the trainers for this slice of combat life were over six feet, like Glenn.

Glenn couldn't possibly get out while tucked up in a ball, but "I knew I was leaving. So I went out in a sitting position and tucked my head in like a turtle and went out feet first.

"I fell free until I approached the clouds. It was time to use the parachute. I'm sure I said this out loud – *I'd better see if the damn thing's going to work* – and I pulled the handle."

The next thing Glenn remembers was literally lifting his head from his chest. "I probably had blacked out from the thrust, the lack of oxygen and being absolutely scared to death.

"Every place I looked was white. I thought, 'I made it! I'm in heaven!' Then I heard a *pop pop pop* noise. Finally I looked over my head and saw my parachute. The popping noise was from my body oscillating underneath and popping the shroud lines.

"Then I broke out of the clouds. I was floating down relatively slowly, and you begin to gather yourself up and think in terms of 'It looks like I might make it. The plane's been destroyed, I didn't get shot. I got out of the darned thing without hitting my head. I pulled the parachute handle and it worked. I'm going to make it.'"

At this point in the retelling of his story to middle-school students, Glenn would pause for effect and add, "Not really."

"There was a very strong wind that day – 50 mph on the ground. As you come down in a parachute, you're moving across the land (almost as fast as) a Piper Cub. So as I'm coming down, I see a river. Oh, hell, I'm going to land in a river. And I don't swim well, especially with a parachute blossomed over me. So that's how it's going to end.

"I kept coming down and then blew on across the river. So, it's going to be all right."

Not really.

"On the other side was a railroad track. There was a darned freight train moving along the track. I figured I'd get plastered to the side of the freight train."

He sailed over the train and into a grove of pine trees.

He'd made it (although not really).

Lt. King, who never had jumped out of an airplane before (and never would again), forgot a piece of jumping instruction from his training: Gentlemen, cross your legs. Caught up in the fierce winds, Glenn landed painfully in a pine tree. "The end of my pelvis was numb for a week or two afterward." In fact, he didn't know if he would be able to father a child until his wife Dottie became pregnant with their first son late in 1951.

Dangling barefooted from the tree (the slipstream had sucked the flight boots right off his feet), Glenn was unable to reach the jackknife in his pocket to cut the shroud lines because the parachute harness was in the way. "I was absolutely weak," he says.

He tried swinging back and forth to dislodge the lines from the branches. "My feet hit the ground and sprung me back up. My feet were now two feet off the ground, and I still couldn't get out of the darned thing."

Help was on the way, however. Three soldiers ran toward Glenn, rifles pointed. "The guy in front blew his whistle. I had my hands above my head, of course. When they saw that I was harmless, they set their rifles against a tree. That's when I motioned to them to cut the shroud lines because the harness was hurting me. The guy pulled out a switch-blade knife and was whittling by my ear. I look over and see a Swastika on his cap. Now I knew where I was."

He would not know until later that the soldier of the Wehrmacht who sliced him down from the pine tree saved his life. Had he been met by a detachment of the Gestapo, Germany's secret police, he knows for certain he would have been shot because they didn't take prisoners. The Wehrmacht did. "From the books I've read since the war, there is no question in my mind the German Army, especially the Luftwaffe, had high respect for what we were doing as flyers, these idiots that were bombing in the daylight."

The German soldiers took their captive to a nearby airbase jail. On the way Glenn spied a Messerschmitt ME-262, the first twin-engine German jet, sitting on the ground. If the Third Reich had had that fighter plane a little earlier, Glenn has read, the air war might have had an entirely different outcome.

Glenn was questioned by a German fighter pilot "who looked a lot like me. Tall, blonde hair, a flyer. He started questioning me in good English: *What time were you shot down? What was your location?* He was trying to confirm a victory for himself."

Protocol for captured American soldiers is to reveal name, rank and serial number. Glenn obliged his interrogator with this information several times, and ultimately was returned to his cell.

It had been about an hour since he had bailed out. It felt much longer.

In bits and pieces, Glenn would learn that the rest of the crew, strangers to him, bailed out in a matter of minutes after he did. The plane exploded and no parachutes were observed, thus giving the Air Corps reason to believe the entire crew had perished. The families would be told their loved ones were missing in action.

In time, the crew would learn that everyone had survived the bailout except the tail gunner, John Nostin, of New Britain, Connecticut. Nostin, who had flown his first combat mission the day before, was dragged to death by his parachute across a plowed field. His family would write to the Kings in Midwest, and later to Glenn, to ask if John had said any last words.

While Glenn never knew the tail gunner or anyone else on Tipton's crew, Mr. and Mrs. King corresponded until the end of the war with Mrs. Kenneth G. Tipton (wife of the pilot), Mrs. Craig (mother of the co-pilot), Mrs. Jack M. Waller (wife of the navigator), Mrs. Glenn Childress (wife of the ball turret gunner), Mrs. Charles Eckert (mother of the waist gunner), Mrs. Frank E. Mang (wife of the radio operator), Nicholas and Anna Nostin (father and sister of the tail gunner) and Mrs. Mabel Slenker (mother of the top turret gunner). *Have you heard anything yet? Surely they are okay, somewhere, trying to get home. We must have faith. What have you heard? I have received a telegram today from the War Department....*

Mrs. King saved all these letters in a cigar box for the day she was sure her boy would return home.

Glenn had only glanced at them until preparing for this book.

From the airbase jail, Glenn joined co-pilot Ed Craig on a truck with two armed guards. Craig's flight suit had been shredded. "You look like you've been fighting wildcats," Glenn told him. Craig recounted his landing in enemy terrain in those 50 mph winds. He, too, had been dragged across a field by his parachute, flipping from one shoulder to the other, and then on to his back. When he cracked his head on something buried in the field, he rolled over onto his belly. When at last he came to a stop, the Germans picked him up and filtered him through interrogation.

Glenn tried to keep calm and maintain a low profile, no easy task for someone his size. The strategy would save his life.

"The thing that scared me is that this one guard spoke about how a sister or daughter or mother had been killed in such and such town. The first thing I did when I got away from the guards, I threw these babies (bombardier wings) as far away as I could." And so, Lt. King became a full-time navigator.

Glenn and Ed were driven to a railroad station. On the floor of the train platform, they ate their first meal in Germany – a square of black bread spread with beet butter – under the noses of two machine guns.

The navigator, 2nd Lt. Jack Maury Waller, of Galveston, Texas, also was captured, and his story would become part of an online database created by researcher J. Kurt Spence, who found 175 POW photographs, including Waller's, at the National Archives in 2007[3]. Spence spent the next four years attempting to put a story with each picture.

Fresh from his bailout of Tipton's B-17, Waller had slung a hunk of firewood over his shoulder and started walking west, Glenn learned after the war. Eventually spotted by a civilian policeman, he was paraded

3 Spence's research is hosted at http://www.fold3.com/profile/jkurtspence/

through the streets of a small town where a bystander threw a brick, hitting him in the face and knocking out a tooth. The wound to his upper lip is clearly visible in the black and white photograph taken at the interrogation center Dulag Luft (Oberursel) and later found by Spence. Waller and Glenn were detained at the same facility but never saw each other.

In the Fall of 2013, Glenn saw Waller's POW picture for the first time. "I would have liked to have known this guy. Obviously he had guts," Glenn observed.

At the interrogation center, Glenn received two things that would save his life: an overcoat and a pair of boots, distributed by the International Red Cross. This would not be the last time the Red Cross saved him.

Hundreds of crewmen were lined up, turning their pockets inside out and undergoing inspection. Ever keen to make sure he was ahead of whatever game needed to be played now, Glenn noticed no one was inspecting footwear, which proved an excellent place to conceal his Sheaffer Flyboy pen and pencil, graduation gifts from Fran. The Germans never gave his boots a glance. (He still has the pencil. The pen was lost during one of his many school presentations.)

Tucked into the shin pockets of his flight suit were cotter keys, pulled from the bombs to arm them prior to their being dropped. Because the Allies had discovered that undetonated bombs were land-ing in Germany with the cotter keys still lodged in the fuses, the order went out for all keys to be returned to base and counted after each mission.

Glenn had a little fun with the guard who would pull one key out, try to decipher the attached tag, put it down, and fish out another. Glenn had about forty cotter keys in his pockets, and kept the guard busy, if not a little confused, for several minutes.

All personal possessions had to be surrendered, so Glenn gave up the watch that had been issued to the officers of the Army Air Corps. The back of it was engraved with "Property of the United States Army

Air Corps," Glenn points out. According to the Geneva Convention, the Germans were entitled to confiscate anything military belonging to their captives.

"I was with a sergeant there, who was also being processed, and they took his watch. I sidled up to him and asked, 'That watch they took from you? Was it an Air Corps hack watch?'"

No, he said, it was a gift from his mother and father.

"Well, I went over to the German guard and said, 'Hey, this watch that you took from me, if you turn it over, it says it's property of the Army Air Corps. You took a watch from this young man. If you turn it over, it doesn't say that on the back. His parents gave him that watch.'"

The guard rifled through the box in front of him, found the sergeant's watch and returned it.

At the Dulag Luft, short for German **Du**rchgangs**lager** der **Luft**waffe (Transit Camp – Air Force), Glenn's fierce face is recorded for all time on the German paperwork written up when he was captured. These pages, brought to Glenn after liberation, have been shown to and handled by hundreds of junior high students in Naperville, Illinois.

Glenn was put into a cell by himself at the Dulag Luft. "The only thing in there was a cot with slats on it, no mattress, and a horse blanket."

The room had an opaque window, through which pistol, rifle and machine gunfire frequently could be heard. "All you can wonder is, are they shooting prisoners? I guess they are. I was there a couple of days, I guess, and then they took me into this officer, a Captain, who told me in an Oxford accent that it was very nice to meet me.

"Of course, as a second lieutenant you don't know too many strategic plans for invading Germany. As a consequence, the depth of his inquiry was pretty minimal," Glenn says.

The exchange lasted less than fifteen minutes. Glenn returned to his unheated cell. No food, no books, nothing to occupy his time. "I lay on the bunk and noticed there were nails in the ceiling, so I started counting them to see what the total was. When I'd finish, I'd do it again, to see if I'd get the same number. That was my amusement."

Once the processing was completed, Glenn and many other American aviators were trucked to a Frankfort train station.

That is where the war began to look a lot different.

"While we were waiting to get on a train, there was a crew of about six burly-looking guys, spitting at us and calling us *schweinehund* (an insult that translates roughly as bastard). Frankly, it scared the devil out of us, even though we were being guarded by these two guys. Who will the guards shoot first, them or us?" Glenn recalls with a tight smile.

The guards grew concerned, however, as these men continued to call out and intimidate the American crewmen. "They took us down into a basement with a light bulb that barely burned the filament. It was just dark. And they held us there until the train came to get us away from those guys.

"Those guys were upset, and they had a lot of reason to be. They were out filling all the holes we'd been making in the rail yard, and it was obvious we were flyboys." The electrical cord dangling from their flight suits was the giveaway.

"The guards had a job to do," Glenn observes, but because they respected the Americans as soldiers, the guards kept their prisoners in the relative safety of the dim basement rather than outside on the platform.

This would not be the last act of respect shown to Glenn and the American flyers.

The POWs were put on a train to a prison camp in Nuremberg, two hours southeast of Frankfurt.

While he had no idea where he was going or what would happen next, Glenn learned after the war that Glenn Childress, the ball turret gunner on the Tipton crew, managed to escape and bring word to the War Department that the crew had bailed out and were now prisoners of the Third Reich.

It would be months before Glenn knew this, of course, and it ate at him that his folks and his brother, Jerry, didn't know what had happened to him.

From the *Casper Star-Tribune*:

First Lt. Glenn W. King, 21, son of Mr. and Mrs. Leslie A. King, Midwest, is reported as missing in action following a flight over Germany on March 2, 1945, according to word received by his parents from the war department.

Lieutenant King was bombardier on a B-17 and had over 20 missions to his credit prior to the report of his missing in action. He was a Member of the Eighth Air Force operating out of England. He had been awarded the Air Medal and Oak Leaf clusters for gallantry in action.

In a letter from a member of his crew who did not go on the mission which ended in disaster, Mr. and Mrs. King learned that the plane was downed near the Russian line, when it ran into intense fighter opposition.

Lieutenant King graduated from the Midwest high school in 1942 and attended Wyoming University at Laramie. He enlisted in the army air corps reserve Dec. 10, 1942. He took training at Columbia, Mo., and his cadet pre-flight at Ellington field, Houston, Tex. He received his wings and commission as a bombardier at Childress field, Texas, April 29, 1944. He arrived in England Sept. 1944.

Glenn, about two years old, was presented with a silver dollar to keep still for the photographer. Circa 1926, Jamestown, North Dakota.

Leslie King, Glenn's father, on a fishing trip, circa 1943.

Alice King with her faithful Cocker Spaniel, Honey, posing in the snow in Colorado on a hunting trip. "She didn't shoot," Glenn says.

Glenn, about age ten, with sidekick Jack, who rode behind his master's bike in a specially designed wagon in order to save wear and tear on his paws.

Glenn next to his Dad's 1941 Oldsmobile. The oil wells of
Midwest are just visible in the background. Circa 1943.

Glenn holds his brother, Jerry, age six.
Mrs. King wrote on the back *Feb. 21,
1943 –Taken as leaving for Service.*

Portrait of 2nd Lt. Glenn W. King taken in May 1944, just after he received his wings and commission from bombardier school in Childress, Texas. This photograph, taken in Casper, Wyoming, was framed and placed in the window of Midwest's drug store alongside scores of other pictures of young men serving in the Armed Forces from the Midwest area.

The Starkel Crew in Tampa, where transition began. Standing left is pilot Robert H. Starkel; co-pilot Henry C. "Hank" Zmudka; navigator Robert G. Poage; and bombardier Glenn W. King. Kneeling left is Charles O. Johnson (waist gunner); Robert L. Phillips (top turret gunner); Dana Sweet (waist gunner); Irving M. Bregman (tailgunner); Wilton "Treetop" Evans (ball turret gunner); and Clayton E. Land, radio operator. Circa 1944.

Navigator Bob Poage and co-pilot Hank Zmudka stand with Glenn on a trip to London, circa 1944. Behind them is one of the four lions guarding the memorial to Horatio Nelson, hero of the Battle of Trafalgar.

"Dottie thought this picture was hilarious," Glenn says. "The fact that we are out there in a bomb shelter, and what do we take with us? Our whiskey." From left, Hank Zmudka, Bob Poage, Howard Tripp, Robert Starkel, Charles Armbruster, and Glenn. The day before Glenn bailed out over Germany, Tripp and Armbruster lost their lives in a mid-air collision.

CHAPTER FIVE

STARVATION

On the train to Stalag XIIID, a POW camp in Nuremberg, Germany, Glenn met soldiers who had been captured trying to liberate Gen. George S. Patton's son-in-law.

Word filtered back on the train that the guys "took the Germans by surprise, liberated the son-in-law and then went around and shot everything up. Then they ran out of gasoline, and everyone got captured," Glenn says. It is, at best, a controversial story in the history books. It was hardly a morale-booster at this stage of the war.

The camp at Nuremberg, enclosed with barbed wire, housed thousands of Allied POWs in unheated barracks. They slept on triple-deck metal bunks with no mattresses. There was little to no food. Starvation was the order of the day. Conditions were filthy, and sanitation was non-existent "They weren't feeding us. We realized we were going down so rapidly, so that we literally lay in our bunks all day long to conserve what energy we had," Glenn says.

Even joking about food was off limits, as Glenn recalls being hollered at by a soldier reclining on another bunk:

"Hey King! Are you busy?"

"No, not really."

"Well, let's go down to the corner and get a hamburger and a shake!"

The whole barracks reared up as one and yelled at the soldier to SHUT UP. "They didn't want to be reminded of food."

As a child, Glenn recalls, his parents, firm believers in thrift and economy, made him eat his peas, which he loathed. "While I was a POW, I could see those damn peas. And hear my Dad say, 'Son, eat those peas. One day, you may wish you had those damn peas.' I never told Dad that story."

Food, if it can be called that, sometimes arrived at the front gate. For those thousands of men, there would be a goat or sheep carcass along with ten loaves of black bread.

"On this one day," Glenn recalls, "one fellow, possibly an officer, just decided he wanted a whole loaf of bread for himself. And he was discovered.

"We knew we were all starving, but someone who would go ahead and steal from his fellow man for his own good is not worth a damn. We ought to just ask the Germans to shoot him. We talked about this.

"Instead, the men conferred and said, 'You know, this guy likes bread real well, so for ten days, the only thing he's going to get is bread and water.' Before that ten days expired, they put us on the forced march to another prison camp at Moosburg, so they rescinded the order."

The carcass-and-bread menu perked up later on with the addition of a sack of beans. "And we thought, 'Oh boy! They're finally going to feed us.' There was a regular kitchen there for us, and we had guys who knew how to cook. They made soup out of the beans.

"When we went down to eat it, you noticed there were little black flecks floating on the top. You'd pick off the flecks with your wooden paddle and knock them on the table. We finally noticed each bean had a black speck. They were weevils, insects. The Germans wouldn't eat it, so they gave it to us. But our cooks said, 'You know guys, we just boiled the devil out of this, so we don't think it'll hurt you. Why don't we go ahead and eat up. It's the most food we've had since we've been here.

"So we ate our soup. Nobody got sick."

Glenn still has the paddle-like spoon that he used to eat whatever came his way. He made it by whittling a scrap of wood with a borrowed "knife" crafted from a nail.

"We were with guys who'd been POWs for a long time, and they had learned the Germans would take anything like a knife away, so they would crawl under the barracks to search out the biggest nail they could find. The bigger the nail, the better. They would work at it until they got it loose from the barracks.

"At Nuremberg, there were a lot of rocks protruding from the soil. They would sit there with this nail and a rock and pound on it day after day to shape it to be like a knife. Then they would hone it on another rock.

"I borrowed one of those knives, found some wood and whittled it into a paddle to eat with, if there was anything to eat."

A watery bowl of soup and a two-inch square of black bread mostly made of sawdust were barely sustaining the men. "I knew I was going down rapidly," Glenn says. "To go to the toilet, you'd learn to get hold of the bedpost because you knew you were going to black out from low blood pressure. So then you'd come to and go about your business. But our organs were shutting down. We didn't have bowel movements."

At night, the British Royal Air Force (RAF) was busy bombing Nuremberg. As the Germans sent up antiaircraft fire, the POWs would listen to the flak as it rained back down to earth, skittering across the roofs of their barracks.

Glenn is not entirely sure at what point the Red Cross made a tiny dent in the vast deprivation that was Nuremberg. But when a truck out of Switzerland delivered five-pound food parcels to camp, it was a pinpoint of hope. "We never got very many of them as a group, and we'd always have to share what was in this parcel. Spam, a can of sardines, tuna fish, a can of oleo margarine, sugar cubes, cigarettes, soap, and dark, dark bitter chocolate – the kind we're supposed to be eating now, but we hated it then. Those were the main ingredients. Very substantial."

One day, Glenn was given a can of tuna. "What was common with the fellas was they would pool themselves and say, 'Let's eat your tuna fish today. We'll eat my sardines tomorrow and the Spam the next day.'"

Glenn thought hard about that can. He'd look at it and think, "You know, I can make it today. I'm feeling okay, so I'm going to save you for tomorrow." Then tomorrow would come, and "I'd get my can of tuna out of my pocket and say, 'I can make it today. I'm going to save you for tomorrow.'"

Everything, he says, was about survival. "That's all you really thought about." But the flyers did what they could to help. "One of our guys came by waving a twenty dollar bill asking for cigarettes. And somebody called out, 'Here!' and tossed him a pack from a Red Cross parcel. 'Keep your twenty.' That was the attitude."

As the prisoners' health deteriorated, Glenn (and everyone else) could see that anyone who went on "sick call" never came back. "That was the last thing you wanted to do."

Even when medical help was provided, it was questionable. A navigator who had bailed out of his plane had broken his arm, which was set by the Germans at a painful angle. "I could never understand at the time why the Germans couldn't set an arm. Until I learned he was Jewish. I concluded the doctor wasn't interested in his having a straight arm."

Everyone's health was in steep decline. Glenn figures his weight, 225 pounds when he was shot down, was well below 180 pounds. He'd been at Nuremberg approximately three weeks. On April 3, 1945, the prisoners learned they were to march to Stalag VIIa in Moosburg, a POW camp approximately 100 miles south toward Austria, not far from the town of Dachau.

There would be hard-won food and exercise on the road, two things entirely absent from camp. The march would save Glenn's life.

"I don't remember the sequence of various things that happened between Nuremberg and Moosburg," Glenn says, "except the first day out and the chickens."

Thousands of men, marching three abreast, filled the streets and villages of southern Germany. All Glenn could see behind him and in front of him were the heads of American soldiers bobbing in formation. Once out in the countryside, edibles were made manifest in the form of chickens. "Guys caught some of these chickens when they locked us up in a farmyard. They cooked and ate them. The next morning, they lined us up and said, 'We know that some of you caught and killed chickens last night. From now on, anyone caught stealing chickens will be shot.' And that was the end of the chicken dinners."

Glenn recalls that a few days into the march, "they passed the word back that the Germans had put together a big batch of soup, and everybody would get a bowl. Well, we stood in the rain all day long, cold, waiting, and moving up just 50 feet once in a great while.

"Finally, it got to be dusk, and the word was passed back that they ran out of soup. So we got nothing."

The farmers' fields, however, were another story. Potatoes, turnips, and wheat became fair "game."

"Every farmyard had a dump yard someplace," Glenn explains. "Somebody was scrambling around and found an old coffee grinder, and we would share that to grind wheat, which we'd stuff in our pockets. Then we'd cook it like a porridge. That was good nutrition."

With a little more food came hope – and ingenuity borne of hunger. In what would be known as the Great Potato Theft, Glenn explains that it was customary for a farmer to build a cellar into the side of a hill, add a door at the front and leave a hole in the top "so he could drive a wagon over the roof and drop off his turnips, potatoes and so on." The harvest accumulated on the cellar floor.

"This one place we went into we found the little cellar, and I went out of there with my pockets stuffed with potatoes, my shirt was stuffed with potatoes, I was going to eat potatoes for a long time. And I like to tell this story because it had more to do with building morale than any other thing – turned out that the farmer discovered what was going on and his potato pile was going down rapidly. He put a lock on the door.

"That night, I looked out about dusk. It was probably not dark enough to be shot if you were outside. There were three guys up on this roof and they had found a stick and some nails. They drove the nails in one end, found a rope and tied it to the other end. They were up there dropping that pole down the hole in the roof and spearing those potatoes, pulling them up one by one and going back to get more.

"That's when I told myself, if they leave us out here in the country, we're going to make it. We'll flat steal the farmers blind."

At night, the guards locked the POWs in farmyards and barns for safekeeping. Campfires were lit for warmth and for cooking. "The word was, don't be caught out after dark or you'll be shot." As far as Glenn knows, no one was shot on the march.

Occasionally, Allied prisoners knocked at the back doors of these farms in the hope of trading something, such as soap, for eggs. Glenn still remembers the phrase: *Sie haben Eier für seife*? "We tried this a few times. The answer was always '*Nicht*.' They didn't want anything to do with us." And the men never found any eggs.

The German guards, Glenn observed, weren't eating much either. If they were near a town, the guards might slip into town for a decent meal, but on the road, come noon, "they'd take out a little container of oleo margarine and a three-inch slice of black bread, and that was it."

March snows had given way to March rain. The wool coats Glenn and many of the others had been provided by the Red Cross were sodden. "They weighed a ton. If I remember correctly, the Germans had us in kind of a forest type area where we could rest and hang up our coats to give them a chance to dry out.

"I had a bug bite, or something, next to my thumbnail that wasn't healing. I was concerned to the extent that I was watching for red streaks going up my arm from infection." The break in the march gave him the opportunity to light a fire and heat water in order to soak his hand throughout the day. By night, it had improved.

Glenn relates that leaflets ordering the men to quit trying to escape were dropped during the march. "You're hampering the war effort when you escape because as soon as you get to our people, they're going to be taking care of you instead of fighting the war," he explains. Rather than being discouraged, Glenn says, the soldiers took it as a sign that the Allies were coming. And soon.

Orders were orders, so surviving – not escaping – was uppermost in his mind. The sound of B-17s flying five miles overhead reminded Glenn of how much he worried for his parents. "It just really gnawed on me that if there was some way I could get word to the guys on that plane to tell Mom and Dad I was okay. That really bothered me." Still does.

Glenn had known no one in the Nuremberg camp, but he did hear about a P-51 Mustang pilot up ahead in the column named Carlson, whose exploits had been part of a pep talk given at Glenn's last briefing at Great Ashfield. Glenn reconnoitered the sea of Americans in hope of meeting up with the pilot, who had surprised a group of German pilot trainees in the air and forced them to land abruptly.

"Apparently, Carlson got a little over-enthusiastic chasing down this one student, and he caught the scoop of his aircraft on a German runway and bellied in. He didn't catch fire nor did he ground loop.

"This is what they told us in this briefing: that he stayed in the plane and called out to the rest of the squadron, 'Get this SOB at 9 o'clock; Get this one at 11!' He stayed in the plane in full view of the fight until his plane started to smolder. The last time anyone saw him, he was running for the woods with the Germans chasing after him. That's what they told us before my last mission."

Hearing talk of this fearless P-51 pilot and his unconventional landing in Germany, Glenn wanted to meet the guy, so he reconnoitered the roadway and finally located him. "I told him the day I was shot down, they told us about how you snagged your scoop."

Carlson confirmed that he was indeed the same pilot.

"And I told him I heard he was being awarded the Distinguished Flying Cross because of it."

Carlson, a man of very few words, just nodded.

Glenn later learned that Carlson had wanted to fly so badly that he joined the Royal Canadian Air Force and ended up flying from England. Then he flew Spitfires with the RAF. When the 8th Air Force finally got to Europe, he joined the Army Air Corps.

(Improbably Glenn would run into Carlson on a street in Santa Monica, California, after the war. "He was still in uniform, wearing the DFC with many clusters. He was about as good as they come, a real leader. There is no way I can stress how unassuming he was. Obviously, a cool cat in a P-51.")

While the POWs were on the march to Moosburg, buses loaded with Germans soldiers were traveling in the opposite direction. "You could see them in there, and their weapons," Glenn says.

Also appearing on the road was a Red Cross eighteen-wheeler, what the prisoners referred to as a White Angel. "They were headed someplace else," Glenn explains, "but the ranking officer told them, 'No one is in any poorer condition than these troops. We're going to unload it *now.*'" The men liberated the truck of its food and distributed it right there on the road.

Outside of Nuremberg, the men were corralled in a railroad yard. "All of a sudden," Glenn recalls, "P-47 fighter bombers – ours – circled over us to make a bomb run on this railroad yard.

"Directly one of them peels off and we all scattered. I was able to fall flat on my belly behind a big ol' tree and as he came in, he's firing his

50 mm machine guns and kicking dirt up on me. There was a big boom and I felt something hit my legs, and I thought I'd been hit.

"Then he obviously discovered things weren't right, seeing all these troops scattering as he came in for his run. So did the other two guys, thank God.

"So as soon as we saw what was happening, we all jumped up and ran into the woods in case they were going to make another run. I jumped up and ran over there too, though I thought I had holes in my legs.

"When I got to the trees, I took a look. What hit me was the mud thrown up when the bomb hit. And that looked awfully good."

Quietly, he adds, "About ten of us were killed that day."

The next day, U.S. Army Col. Darr Hayes Alkire, commanding officer of the march, sent word through the lines of soldiers that by running, "We behaved like Germans. If this happens again, we're not going to run, we're going to stand in the roadway and wave something white.

"Sure enough, the next day we had two of our own P-51s circling over us. One of them peeled off and came in, and as he crossed the stream of guys ahead of me, I wasn't looking down any gun barrels, but the guys in front of me were. No one broke and ran." The story is still difficult for Glenn to tell.

As the pilot crossed over the sea of prisoners in the roadway, he circled and flew at the height of a telephone pole. "I literally saw him in the cockpit signaling OK with his hand, telling us everything's okay."

The hundreds of Air Force men on the march immediately recognized who was doing the buzzing, and shouted "'Hell! That's one of our recon outfits! They're taking pictures of us!'

"From then on, every morning, and if you'd had a watch you could have set it, at 8 o'clock you had two P-51s, circling overhead."

Things were, as they say, looking up.

Details about the march from Nuremberg to Moosburg are described on a website created by researcher Greg Hatton (www.B24.

net). According to Hatton, on April 9, 1945, "the column reached the Danube, which Col. Alkire flatly refused to cross, since it meant exceeding the 20-kilometer a day (marching) limit. With his refusal, the Germans lost complete control of the march and POWs began to drop out of the column almost at will. The guards, intimidated by the rapid advance of the American Army, made no serious attempt to stop the disintegration. The main body of the column reached Stalag VIIa (Moosburg) on 20 April, 1945."

About all anyone needs to know about Moosburg is that on April 29, 1945, when Gen. George S. Patton liberated the camp of more than one hundred thousand prisoners, he surveyed the emaciated men and unspeakable conditions and said, "I'm going to kill these sons-of-bitches for this."[4]

Glenn and the men from Nuremberg were among the lucky ones. They had foraged for food during their nearly three weeks on the road. They were in much better shape, relatively speaking, than the guys who already had been starving for a very long time in Moosburg.

One of the newspaper stories at the time told how an American soldier liberated his brother from Moosburg. (Mrs. King had clipped that story, too.) Sixty-nine years later, Glenn would watch the liberation films made by the 166th Signal Photographic Company, on his computer monitor. That day in April, however, he was frantically looking for someone to get a letter out to his family and not having much luck.

Glenn had managed to cadge a blank V-mail form from somebody and scrawled a note to his parents to reassure them that he was alive. But how does one post a letter from the heart of wartime Germany? As American soldiers were tramping through the camp, Glenn got the attention of a captain. "I went up to him and said 'I've got a V-mail here. Would you mail this for me? This tells my parents that I'm alive.'"

---

4 Donald L. Miller, *Masters of the Air* (Simon & Schuster Paperbacks, 2006), 505

The captain used some colorful language, mostly about being asked to do something, until Glenn leaned in and said, "Look, this doesn't mean a damn to you, it doesn't mean a damn to me. But it does to somebody else." Glenn shoved the V-mail in the man's front pocket and said, "Mail the damn thing!"

May 1, 1945 Germany

Dearest Mom, Dad and Jerry,

I'm hoping this finds you all in the best of health and I also hope you haven't been worrying too much about me being M.I.A.

I'm O.K. and feeling fine. Nothing has happened to me – not even as much as a scratch.

We have been liberated and are very happy not to be P.O.W.s any longer. They tell us we should be in the states in at least 3 weeks and I hope they're right as I'm really looking forward to being with you.

I'm running out of space so I'll just hope I can beat this letter home.

So long,
Your loving son,
Glenn xxxxxx
Hi Jerry xxx

After liberation, the men remained in camp a full week. "We got absolutely no food during that time," Glenn says. "Our front-line troops were moving so fast, they didn't have anything for us. The only way you'd get something was if by chance a guy walking through the barracks, looking for someone from home, might slip you some K-rations. But barring that, there was nothing for us to eat."

While waiting to be evacuated, a bunch of the former POWs raided the Moosburg camp office and brought Glenn his induction papers from the interrogation center. He has them to this day. And while they have faded to an odd orange color, the furious face of Glenn W. King, age 21, is caught for all time on its pages.

While they were out scavenging, the men raided a silverware chest and brought bits and pieces back to their friends to share. Glenn picked up a spoon and a knife, which he still has. The swastikas imprinted on the handles are faint but still visible.

Glenn also held on to that tuna can because, well, you never know.

"Some of the guys had more of a spirit of, I don't know, discovery. See what they could find, a German Luger or food. I didn't scrounge for souvenirs because I felt there was some exposure to that. But the other thing was all the time I was a POW, I tried not to do anything to get noticed because of my size. I tried to stay hid. I only wanted to see tomorrow."

One thing Glenn did notice was "the pallor on the faces of those frontline troops. After the war, I figured out they had to be coming from Dachau (thirty miles southwest of Moosburg). It wasn't normal to see a garrison of our soldiers look the way they looked."

The deprivations of those imprisoned in Germany and the depravity of their captors were just beginning to be publicized. Patton and the Third Army had a front row seat to the horrors perpetrated by the Nazis. Glenn would be one of many witnesses.

CHAPTER SIX

"AND IF OUR GLENN IS SPARED, HE IS THINKING OF US."

Waiting for word about someone in 1945 meant exactly that – waiting on the written word sent by letter or telegram. In Midwest, only company supervisors like Mr. King had telephones. (They were only to be used for company business. Given the tenuous circumstances of his son's life, the Kings' phone was definitely used to receive calls of support.)

On March 21, 1945, the Kings received a telegram from J. A. Ulio, Adjutant General, stating, "The secretary of war desires me to express his deep regret that your son, Sec. Lt. Glen (sic) W. King has been reported missing in action since March 2nd over Germany."

It is but one of a great many letters and notices that Alice King saved in the sure knowledge that her son would return safely.

She kept a sheet of paper to record all who visited in those early days. One of the first names on her list was that of Mrs. McKenna, the school principal. "She was the one I remember Mom pointing out early in my return, that she had come over and talked with them from the high school," Glenn recalls. Mrs. McKenna told the Kings: "Glenn's going to be all right. He's got a level head on his shoulders. He'll figure it all out."

To this day, it is a kindness that Glenn has not forgotten.

Glenn had not read every letter or name on the visitor's list until this book was being written. It has not been easy to reflect on those names and the feelings they evoke.

Mrs. Volkmer, a neighbor; Mrs. Burch across the street; Mrs. Hershey, a good friend; Bertha Roberts, four years older than Glenn; Mrs. Bailey ("I went all the way through school with their only son, a little hellion!"); Mrs. Morris; Rev. Taylor; Mrs. Roy Miller; Rev. Campbell; Mrs. Scott from across the street ("I grew up with her son and two daughters"); Mrs. Daley by telephone ("We went deer hunting with Mr. Daley"); Aunt Mea by telephone; the Coggshells, very close friends; Mark Crawford; Mrs. Warburton; Mrs. Okee Kinion; the Hersheys, good friends; the Lambs, very good friends; Mrs. Bailey; Mrs. Daley, again; the Coggshells again; Mrs. Crawford; the Lambs, again; Mrs. Kinion by telephone.

On April 19, Miss Dilly, Miss Nellie Simpson and Miss Bennett, Glenn's former teachers, stopped in. ("I would never have thought Miss Simpson would come out. She never showed any compassion for anyone!"); the Mahaffeys, close friends; Mable Sinadin ("Her son Johnny was a POW of the Japs."); the Lambs, again; Martin Brunck by telephone; Zola and Gene.

On May 8, Henry Zmudka, Glenn's co-pilot, by phone. On May 9, Mrs. Hosking and Miss Simmons, teachers, and Fran Jones' aunt.

Nearly all of Midwest wrote letters, dozens visited, and a few telephoned. Telegrams arrived. The prayers and heartfelt words of consolation wrapped the Kings in such loving kindness that it still is almost too much for Glenn to take in. While he had glanced at a few of the letters upon his return, it took two days and some steel to power through their reading sixty-eight years later.

The outpouring from the community to support his parents and brother when he could not is today a source of consolation. "That was the thing that bothered me the most because I knew it was just shattering them, not knowing what had happened to me."

From Jackson, Wyoming, Bobby Cooke's sister, Madolyn, wrote:

> *I was so sorry to hear about the sad news you received of Glenn. It seems so hard to believe and I know all too well the heavy weight that is in your hearts. You do have one consolation though so many boys previously reported missing have been found again.*
>
> *Please know that my prayers are with you and that you soon will have more encouraging news.*
>
> *In understanding sympathy,*
> *Madolyn Cooke*

Bobby, Glenn's high school pal from football and co-conspirator of the famous road swerve, had lost his life the previous December. He had been serving on the USS Hull, a Navy destroyer that sank during a typhoon near the Caroline Islands.

For Glenn today, the letters that Mrs. King saved eloquently evoke the home front during his forced separation from all whom he loved.

⸻

385th Bombardment Group (H)
Office of the Chaplain
8 March 1945

> *Dear Mr. King,*
> *In times such as this, I hardly know just what to say because I only know in part your distress and anxiety. But I do feel that you can find courage, comfort and hope as the Psalmist found when he said, "I will lift up mine eyes unto the hills from which cometh my help. My help cometh from the Lord which made the heavens and the earth. The Lord shall preserve thy going out and thy coming in from this time forth and for evermore."*

Since your son, 2nd Lt. Glenn W. King, 0-722726, has been reported missing in action, we have been anxiously waiting for some word. Glenn was a fine man, a good soldier, and a man of good character. I have great confidence in him and the other men who know what to do in an emergency such as this, and in faith, hope and prayer, we anxiously wait for good news.

Glenn's Commanding Officer, Col. George Y. Jumper, the Commanding General, Eighth Air Force, and the men of this station extend to you in these hours of distress our deepest sympathy. If I can assist you at any time, feel free to call upon me.

Sincerely,
James O. Kincannon,
Chaplain (Capt.) USA
Group Chaplain

March 21, 1945 telegram

Mr. Les King:

The Secretary of War desires me to express his deep regret that your son Sec. Lt. Glen (sic) *W. King has been reported missing in action since March 2nd over Germany.*

If further details or other information are received you will be promptly notified.

J. A. Ulio
The Adjutant General

Wednesday, March 21ˢᵗ (1945)

>*Dear Mr. and Mrs. King,*
>
>*As you may or may not know, I'm Glenn's navigator. We were told not to write for several weeks, hence, my delay in writing you.*
>
>*I'd like to tell you all I know regarding Glenn's mission – in the hope that, if at all possible, I can ease your minds somewhat and give you some hopeful information. To begin with, our crew wasn't flying that day, except Glenn. He was flying with a new crew. The mission was one pretty close to the Russian lines. As you may or may not know, our group was hit by fighters around the target area. Four planes were hit pretty bad, among them Glenn's. His plane was last seen dropping behind the formation and losing altitude. The plane appeared under perfect control.*
>
>*From the reports of all who saw it, they probably had to abandon the plane. In which case, it was agreed by all that they had the time necessary to do it and then some.*
>
>*The general concensus (sic) from those flying is that they all bailed out and will either be picked up as war prisoners or made their way to the Russian lines. We're all hoping and praying that one of these happened. That is about all the information I could gather from those flying.*
>
>*I know this explanation has been rather blunt and not too easy to take. I think though that you would like to know all that did happen, so I hope you'll excuse my rather blunt explanation.*
>
>*Everyone who saw the incident gives them all the very best chance for safety, which is very promising, I believe.*
>
>*By the way, Glenn became a first lieutenant the 14ᵗʰ of March.*
>
>*If at any time I receive any more news at all, I'll notify you immediately! If you receive any more news also I'd*

appreciate knowing also. If you do, you could write to me at my home in Tampa, Florida. I hope to have completed my tour and be on my way home in a few weeks.

If I can tell you anything more in any way, please write me and I'll do my best. We're all very interested in helping in any way if at all possible. Glenn was perhaps the most popular boy in our squadron and we all hope and pray with you that he is safe and well. Please write if I can be of any more help in any way. I only hope this has been of some hope and assurance to you.

Sincerely,
Bob (Poage, navigator on the Starkel crew)

⸺⸻⸺

23 March 1945

Dear Mr. King:
This letter is to confirm my recent telegram in which you were regretfully informed that your son, Second Lieutenant Glenn W. King, 0722726, has been reported missing in action over Germany since 2 March 1945.

I know that added distress is caused by failure to receive more information or details. Therefore, I wish to assure you that at any time additional information is received, it will be transmitted to you without delay, and, if in the meantime no additional information is received, I will again communicate with you at the expiration of three months. Also, it is the policy of the Commanding General of the Army Air Forces upon receipt of the "Missing Air Crew Report" to convey to you any details that might be contained in that report.

The term "missing in action" is used only to indicate that the whereabouts or status of an individual is not immediately known. It is not intended to convey the impression that the case is closed. I wish to emphasize that every effort is exerted continuously to clear up the status of our personnel. Under war conditions this is a difficult task as you must readily realize. Experience has shown that many persons reported missing in action are subsequently reported as prisoners of war, but as this information is furnished by countries with which we are at war, the War Department is helpless to expedite such efforts.

The personal effects of an individual missing overseas are held by his unit for a period of time and are then sent to the effects Quartermaster, Kansas City, Missouri, for disposition as designated by the soldier.

Permit me to extend to you my heartfelt sympathy during this period of uncertainty.

Sincerely yours,

J.A. Ulio
Major General
The Adjutant General

March 23, 1945
Sheridan Wy

Dear Brother and family,
We are very sorry to learn of Glenn's terrible danger and join you in hopes and prayers for his safety.

Waiting, at a time like this, is an awfully tense thing. I wish we could do something to make it easier for you.

We have been holding our breath, as it were, ever since we learned he was working over enemy territory. Of course the B17 is a very tough and safe ship, and with the added protection of the flak suits, a man has an excellent chance of getting away from a ship. With the fronts closing in so rapidly the Germans will be careful in the treatment of captured Americans.

Mr. Becker, the music director in our H.S. had his son reported missing and it took about 6 weeks for official notice of his safety as a prisoner to reach the father.

Officers receive better treatment as prisoners than do enlisted men, which makes the picture somewhat brighter.

Somehow it's hard to believe that Glenn is missing and one can't help feeling that somehow that he will turn up as a temporary PW – and we can only hope and pray for his safe return.

You have all our sympathy.

Affectionately,
Bill and Alice (brother and sister-in-law of Leslie King)

March 25, 1945
Jamestown, ND

Dear Leslie, Alice and Gerald,
We are so sorry to hear this sad news of Glenn. How we hope and pray he might have escaped with his life someway.

You have my deepest sympathy in these dark hours, also Mrs. Friedholm (Glenn's maternal grandmother). He was so dear to us all.

We are glad to hear that Loraine is with you at this time.

Yes, this war is an awful thing and seems so useless if people would consider each others' rights to begin with. I was busy all day yesterday so did not get to answer this. But have had you on my mind a lot and hope you are well. . . .

Love and best wishes to all,
Mother (Mary King, Glenn's grandmother)

———

March 25
Lincoln, Neb.

Dear Mr. and Mrs. King,
Mother wrote me the news today that Glenn was "missing in action." Please do not give up hope! Remember that there is always someone far more powerful than we are watching over them. My greatest comforting thought I might give to you is to tell you to read the 91st Psalm.

To me it makes the waiting more bearable and keeps hope alive for their safe return.

Reid had told me of so many precautions and instructions that would help them to escape in case of a "forced landing" that I can only give you words of encouragement. It is all so many of us have these days . . . .

In case this report was a false one I, too, would be very happy because news of each day being safe, especially one you know, adds to the brighter things of Life.

May God bless your family and help you all.

Sincerely,
Nora Thompson

March 25, 1945
104ᵗʰ Infantry Division

Dear folks and Gerald,

I was talking to a correspondent in a small town one day and since he wanted boys from Iowa (he had a syndicate for that state. I asked him if he had even seen anyone from Wyoming. Imagine my surprise when he said a Lieutenant here in the same group I was attached to was from Casper. He was Lt. Carlson, and we had a short chat where on our reminiscences he said he knew the whole King family well. I promised him I would write Glenn and let him know. From what I could find out he is a communications officer and is well liked and capable. A grand combination!

I am glad to hear Glenn is safe and well and has so many missions behind him. He's a good boy.

I better close now and get down to business. I hope it is poor.

Sincerely,
Timer
(Pfc. Charles F. Moses)

(Timer, a great high school pal and one of Glenn's guests at his 18th birthday party, was not aware that Glenn had been captured. This speaks to how slow communication was in 1945.)

March 26, 1945

> Dear Mr. and Mrs. King and Jerry,
> I've wanted to write you before but have been trying to think of something to say which might lessen your anxiety and grief. But words are empty things at best.
> Glenn is so resourceful and strong that given any kind of a fighting chance he will come out on top.
> You know, when events move as rapidly as they now are in Europe we can't help but wonder why it takes so long for information about our loved ones to reach us.
> I'd like to say that our thoughts, hopes and prayers for good news about one of Midwest High School's finest men are continuous. I know Raymond would join me in wishing you comfort.
>
> Sincerely,
> Lucille McKenna

Friday night
March 30, 1945

   Dear Mrs. King
   I cannot find words to tell you how very, very sorry I am to hear that Glenn is missing over Germany. It's hard to believe – of course, I realize that every time he went on a mission there was that possibility that he would not return. Glenn didn't mention the number of missions he had completed very often, although some time back he said he had sixteen to his credit. And then I remember in one of his recent letters he said the more missions the better – that way he could get them over with, and come home. Bless him.
   Well, there is every chance in the world that he is a prisoner – my prayers go with yours, Mrs. King, that he is safe and unhurt. Glenn is such a grand boy. He has to be all right.
   It's hard not to be bitter about all this – I find myself asking why it is that those who start wars, and all the sorrow which go with them, never fight them. It's always fine, decent boys like Glenn who are called upon to risk their lives – it's not fair . . . .
   It was kind of you to write to me. Waiting is so difficult – I shall be thinking of you, and hoping that you have good news soon. Dad and mother send their sympathy – we are all concentrating that Glenn is safe somewhere.

   Sincerely,
   Jean Leach
   Beaumont, TX

March 30, 1945
Midwest

Dear Mr. and Mrs. King.

My heart prompts me to do what I haven't the courage to do otherwise. So little is there to say at such a time. I want you to know I'm thinking of you every minute. Feeling heavy hearted and yet feeling, too, that Glenn is coming back. That feeling has persisted from the beginning and I'll be so happy when the Gov. says he is safe. No matter in what hands he may be you know it can't be for long. Our armies are sailing thru and he will be liberated very shortly.

Glenn was such a fine boy, a credit to himself, his family and most certainly his country. You have every right to be proud of him and it will be a great day when we hear he's safe.

We are praying for him, that he may return to you safely.

Sincerely,
Helen Connors

⸙

April 2, 1945
Jamestown, N Dak

Dear folks,

I haven't any special news to write but keep thinking of you during this solemn Easter Season dedicated to hope and faith which seems to bring to mind all our loved ones. And we know if our Glenn is spared, he is thinking *of us. And we do pray and hope he is all right somewhere. Our forces and allies are sure making things count in Germany now but it is still questionable just how it will come out . . . .*

I hope that you are well and pray that our Heavenly Father may comfort and Bless you in these anxious dreary days of waiting.

As ever with love,
Mother (Mary King)

———

April 4, 1945
5 p.m.
Casper, Wy
Tuesday Afternoon

Hi folks

I just had a "reading" from Irene and must tell you what she said about Glenn. I made certain specific wishes concerning him – wished to be shown if he was a prisoner, if he was suffering – if he had enough food – if we would hear from him soon etc. According to the cards and Irene's "intuition" or whatever it is, he is a prisoner. He has not been injured but when he landed (she said he had bailed out – and we had not told her of Pogue's letter) he pulled a "leader" in his neck and it is sort of stiff – he rubs the back of his neck a lot.

He also is nauseated – caused by nerves and worry. He is trying desperately to get a message out through some officer but has been unsuccessful. It may be quite some time before you get word from him. He is getting enough to eat – and may be doing some kind of work. He is trying very hard to send you a message mentally. He said that if you could just stop worrying about him and absolutely know he is alright it would help him immeasurably. She also said that he is very disgusted and disappointed to be out of the fight. She made the remark that he is very tenderhearted but tries not to let anyone know it. But there were no bad cards around him except for his worry about you and your worry about him.

She is confident that he is absolutely all right. And that is about all. She said he comes through to her so clearly every time she thinks about him – it must be because he is concentrating on sending his message through. All in all it sounds very good, doesn't it? And it certainly sounds like Glenn, doesn't it?

Lots of love,
Lorry
PS I just remembered something else she said – that there was someone with Glenn – a friend. Must have been one of the boys who bailed out with him.

(Glenn says his first cousin Lorraine Easton, known as Lorry, was "quite a card." In fact, she lived with the Kings in Midwest for two years while Glenn was in high school. While her Tarot card reader missed the mark on nearly everything, she was entirely accurate about his worry for his parents and Jerry. It was unceasing.)

81

April 7th, 1945

> *Dear Mr. and Mrs. King,*
>
> *At last I have a little more news for you. And it's good news!*
>
> *Right now I'm at an R.C.D. (possibly a Red Cross Depot) awaiting a ride home. I went through processing today and ran across a familiar boy – he was a member of one of the crews that went down the same way and place that Glenn did. He'd been liberated by Patton a week or so ago.*
>
> *He couldn't give me much definite information but he did tell me Glenn was a P.W., when I asked him about it. He couldn't tell me where he was or anything like that as they'd been sent to different camps. So possibly before long you'll be hearing from him. I certainly hope so!*
>
> *I imagine Glenn's in a camp in central Germany some- where. Or maybe even liberated by now. Let's certainly hope so.*
>
> *I don't know when I'll get my ride home. Probably be several weeks. So maybe I'll run across some more infor- mation. If I do I'll write you right away about it.*
>
> *Hope you'll also let me know if you hear anything.*
>
> *As ever,*
> *Bob*

(Glenn notes, "Bob Poage was a great guy and an outstanding navi- gator, even if he didn't drink, or much, anyway.")

April 9, 1945

> *Dear Sir,*
>
> *I'm writing this to pass on a bit of information I know you will be very glad to hear. Today one of the gunners on Glen's (sic) crew was fortunate enough to return to the base after escaping from a German prison camp. I am not at liberty to reveal any details, however, I talked to this fellow personally and can tell you that Glen is safe and well – but a prisoner of war. All but one man of the crew are safe.*
>
> *To say the least, we were all very happy to receive this swell news. The other three officers (on Lt. Starkel's crew) have left for home and the enlisted men will leave soon. If we receive any further news of Glen we will write at once. Hope this news finds you well and trust it will indeed make you happy.*
>
> *Sincerely Yours,*
> *Lewis A. Smith, a friend of Glenn's*

Saturday April 14th

> *Dear Mr. and Mrs. King,*
>
> *I received your nice letter today quite by accident. As you know, I'm not at our base any longer . . . . (someone) told me that they were taking most of the prisoners to Nuremburg, and that included Glenn and the rest of the crew. Nuremburg (maybe Nurnburg – I guess they're spelled either way) is, as you know, not far from our lines.*

So I hope with you that Glenn will be liberated shortly. If he is still there he should be because the Germans are backing up so fast, they haven't time to move the PWs with them. As you've probably read, quite a large number already have been liberated.

I forgot to mention in my last letter that Lt. Zmudka, our co-pilot, had mailed a package to you containing some of Glenn's belongings. I don't know if he enclosed a letter or not.

I hope, shortly after you receive this letter, to be back in the States. So if you receive any more news, it would reach me quicker I believe at my home address. And I sincerely hope you hear from him soon.

Thanks again for your wonderful letter.

With best wishes,
Bob (Poage)

———

April 16, 1945

We know there is no happiness as long as dear Glenn is not heard. But news should come through since they are liberated now.

Love,
Mother (Mary King)

———

April 19, 1945

> *Dear Mrs. King,*
>
> *First of all I would like to explain that I am Henry Zmudka's sister and that we received today the letter you sent to my brother. When the letter got to England, they sent it back to us – so I guess my brother isn't there anymore since he didn't get the letter.*
>
> *It's been three weeks since we heard from him and in his last letter he wrote that he had finished his missions and was coming home on furlough. So I figure that he must be on his way home.*
>
> *In the excitement my dad opened your letter by mistake – I hope you will forgive that. But in a way I am glad he opened it because I know how anxious you must be to hear a little news of your son and by now you must be wondering why my brother doesn't answer your letter. I'll send him your letter as soon as I know of his whereabouts and I'm sure he will write to you and let you know as soon as he can, what he possibly can. I hope and pray that he can tell you some good news.*
>
> *I can't express how sorry we were to read of your son being reported missing, and we hope and pray that soon you get news that he is safe.*
>
> *I hope I hear from my brother soon so I can forward your letter to him so he can write to you. Hoping that your prayers will be answered soon.*
>
> *Miss Irene Zmudka*

(Hank Zmudka, Bob Poage and Bob Starkel, the officers of Glenn's original crew, would complete their tour of thirty-five combat missions.

The average Air Corps completion rate was fifteen. The Starkel crew most definitely had defied the odds.)

April 22, 1945
Sheridan Wy

> *Dear Alice and Leslie –*
> *We were so happy to receive your letter and to know that Glenn is known to be alive. My, but it was so nice his buddies wrote to you to let you know he had landed safely. My, I do so hope you can hear from him soon. The anxiety is so awful. Surely, there have been more American boys liberated by now, for as fast as United States troops have been closing in around Berlin. We both hope that Glenn is among those liberated.*
> *Last week on the radio I heard 285,000 of our boys were released from prison camps. Perhaps Glenn was, too. I just can't help but feel you will hear from him soon.*
>
> *Love from,*
> Bill and Alice (William and Alice King, Leslie's brother and sister-in-law)

April 25, 1945
La Mesa, Calif.

> *Dear Folks,*
> *Hi!! Received your grand letter with the <u>wonderful</u> news about Nen t'other day. There are no words adequate*

to express my feelings about his safety, but let it suffice to say I made an awful mess of my mascara when I read your letter. . . .

Love,
Lor (Lorraine, Glenn's first cousin, referencing Glenn's family nickname)

April 30, 1945
Jamestown, N. Dak

Dear Folks

We were very glad to receive your letter, telling of the news you hear about Glenn, and the way the allies and our forces are going after everything in their path. We are praying and hopeful that Glenn may be one of the fortunate ones to be already liberated. It is so good to know that he was safe and well at that time and so kind of these soldier boys to let you know. It does seem that German Warlords would know enough to give up now.

The loss of our president was a great shock and possibly a loss as well, but our new one seems to be doing well so far. . . .

Nelson (her son) *killed two pheasants in his drive with the car lately. We told him he and the pheasants must have an agreement someway when meat is so hard to get.*

Write us soon again.

Love as ever,
Mother (Mary King)

From the Casper Star-Tribune:

Prisoners at Stalag 7A Found in Good Condition

With the U.S. 14th Armored division, May 1 (AP) – In high spirits, 50,000 Americans, half of them air force officers, almost mobbed 14th armored division tankmen today in one of the wildest liberations ever witnessed in Germany.

The Americans were among 130,000 Allied prisoners – including 37 high-ranking officers – freed at Stalag 7A and in the towns around Moosburg where the Germans had the biggest concentration of prisoners in Germany.

In contrast to the starvation conditions prevailing in the other liberated camps, the prisoners in the Moosburg area for the most part were in good physical condition. This was due to the presence among the prisoners of a number of Allied officers, including many colonels.

Another factor contributing to their well-being was the nearness of Switzerland, from whence the International Red Cross was able to provide food parcels without encountering too great transportation difficulties.

At Stalag 7A in Moosburg, where 37,000 prisoners including 14,891 Americans were kept, there were 175,000 Red Cross food packages on hand when the camp was liberated.

(Glenn reiterates that there was no food in the area of the camp where he was because the captives had arrived in the last weeks of the war and were living on the perimeter.)

May 3, 1945
New Britain, Conn.

> Dear Mr. King,
> I am writing you this letter with the hope that you might have heard from your son, Lt. Glenn King, himself or that you might have received word that your son is no longer missing.
> My son, Sgt. John Nostin, was the tail gunner on the missing bomber and as yet I have had no word from him or from any other sources that he is no longer missing.
> I did receive a letter from Headquarters Army Air Forces informing me how the plane was damaged by the enemy and how it fell out of formation and disappeared into the clouds. I also received a list of the missing men and the names and address of their next of kin.
> I would appreciate it very much if you could give me any more information concerning the missing boys and their plane.
>
> Sincerely,
> Nicholas Nostin

May 13, 1945

> Dearest Mom, Dad and Jerry,
> I sure hope that by now you have heard that I'm all right. I'm now at Le Havre, France, and should soon be on my way home.

I'm still in class "A" shape and really enjoying G.I. chow.

I understand that we're to get 60 day leaves and I'm sure planning on a celebration – O.K.

Before I run out of space Mom, I want to wish you the Happiest Mother's Day ever and that I can soon give you all those big kisses. I'm behind.

So long – Your loving son,
Glenn xxxxxx
Hi Jerry xxxx

May 14, 1945

Dear Mr. and Mrs. King

I received a letter from the War Department listing your son Glenn as a member of my husband's crew. My husband has been missing since March 2. Will you please let me know if you receive the same news of your son. . . . I do know that Sgt. Glen R. Childress, the ball turret gunner, is back at base since April 9. I hope the War Department made a mistake and your son is safe. Please let me know if you receive any news.

Mrs. Kenneth G. Tipton

(This was one of four letters the wife of pilot Kenneth Tipton wrote to the Kings.)

May 15, 1945
York, PA

Dear Sir,
Since your son was a member of the same crew as my
son, Rodger C. Maul, I am writing you this good news,
hoping you have heard the same.
The Red Cross representative came to see me today at
noon, told me they had just received news that my son has
been located and is healthy and well, did not say where he
is. So I pray you too will be as happy as me soon.

Yours respectfully,
Mrs. Mabel Slenker

⁕

May 17, 1945
Baltimore, 29 MD

Dear Mr. King,
I hope you have received good news about your son,
2nd Lt. Glenn W. King. I received a letter from my son,
Sgt. Charles C. Eckert, waist gunner on the B29 (sic) that
was reported missing since March 2. He was a prisoner
of war and had recently been released. Charles expects to
return to the States around the 25th of this month. I hope
you too have received word of your son's safety.

Sincerely,
Emma R. Eckert

⁕

May 17
St. Louis, Mo

> *Dear Mrs. King*
> *I am writing this letter with the hope that you might have heard from your son 2ⁿᵈ Lt. Glenn W. King, himself or that you might have received words he is no longer missing.*
>
> *I have received a telegram from the war dept. that my husband, Sgt. Glenn Childress, reported back on duty April 9 and also two letters from him but he didn't mention any of the crew, how or where they went down.*
>
> *I sincerely hope you have received word of your son by now and I feel sure he will turn up.*
>
> *Sincerely,*
> *Mrs. Childress*

May 19, 1945
Western Union

> *LESLIE A. KING*
> *THE SECRETARY OF WAR DESIRES ME TO INFORM YOU THAT YOUR SON 2/LT KING GLENN W. RETURNED TO MILITARY CONTROL DATE UN REPORTED*
>
> *J.A. ULIO THE ADJUTANT GENERAL*

May 21, 1945
Chattanooga, Tenn

> *Dear Mrs. King*
>
> *Thanks a lot for your nice letter. It sure makes me feel better.*
>
> *I received a letter from Sgt. Glenn R. Childress' wife and she has two letters from him dated April 1-10. Also a wire from the War Department saying he reported back to headquarters April 9th. Also a letter from Mrs. Slenker saying she had news from Sgt. Roger C. Maul*
>
> *I haven't heard anything from my husband yet.*
>
> *Mrs. Waller, wife of Lt. Jack M. Waller, called me tonight saying she had heard the plane exploded in mid-air. Then I told her of your letter and also of Sgt. Childress' return and about the letter I had from Mrs. Childress. She was so glad to get the news. Said her news was delayed because they thought Jack was home. So they must be on their way home. They told her no one got out of the plane. But that has been proved wrong for Sgt. Childress is back and he knew more about what did happen than the other fellows in the formation.*
>
> *Did he say who the unfortunate one was? I want to know if it was my husband or not. I might just as well receive it from someone other than the war department. They are so blunt with it. So please if you hear any further news let me know at once. I'll let you know as soon as I hear any,*
>
> *I do hope you have good news.*
>
> *Sincerely,*
> *Mrs. Kenneth G. Tipton*

May 21, 1945
Galveston, Texas

> *Dear Mr. King*
>
> *My husband, Jack M. Waller, was the navigator on your son's plane. I have intended to write to you since receiving your address from the War Department to ask if you have had any news from your son.*
>
> *I have received nothing official. However, Mrs. Craig, the co-pilot's mother, did write that she had heard from her other son, stationed in the Atlantic, that all the crew got out of the plane.*
>
> *Then yesterday, Mrs. Mang, the radio operator's wife, called to tell me she had a telegram from her husband. He was in the States and would be home before the end of the month.*
>
> *I suppose Mrs. Slenker and Mrs. Childress have written to you about hearing from their boys.*
>
> *So that leaves six to be accounted for. If you have heard or do hear from your son, would you please let me know? If you could call me collect, I'd appreciate it so much! Our phone is 4774-Galveston.*
>
> *I do hope that you have heard something. Surely our boys could have come thru if three did!*
>
> *Wishing you the best news and hoping to hear from you.*
>
> *Most Sincerely,*
> *Oraleee B. Waller*

22 May 1945
550ᵗʰ Bombardment Squadron (H)
Office of the Commanding Officer

Dear Friend King,

Naturally I was tickled to hear from you and to know that you are ok. We had heard lots of rumors and stories, and we didn't know whether you'd turn up or not. Imagine you have some pretty good stories to tell, and I'd like to be back there in Wyoming listening to them.

Your boys (Starkel and crew) *all finished up and went home, and they've no doubt gotten in touch with you. It was a sad night around here when you didn't come back – Starkel especially felt bad – got drunk and still felt bad. Now if we'd only not lost those 2 the day before you went down, we'd be all right. Incidentally, only the tail gunner* (Jones) *on Armbruster's crew got out. You probably saw a story on him – he was trapped in the tail when it broke off, and he just sat down and smoked a cigarette waiting for it to crash. A good man.*

Well – to get after your questions. You are no longer a low-down second lieut. Par 10, SO 73, 8ᵗʰ AF, 14 March 1945 made you a 1ˢᵗ lt. No copy is available here for you but your 201 file has gone forward and you'll just have to sweat out that extra pay till it gets to you – or you can write the Adjutant Gen, WDC and probably get a copy.

I picked up your personal clothes with my own two hands – with help from Davidow and a couple of the others. The stuff was forwarded to Effects QM, UK, APO 507, US Army. It should be forwarded from there to Kansas City QM Depot and from there you'll be informed. However, it might take considerable time. If you want to do any *checking, you can write direct, but I imagine they're sending everything along as fast they can.*

By the way, we found no money at all in your stuff. If you were carrying it, you can put in a claim to the govt for stuff taken from you by the enemy – watch, pen, money, etc. We found quite a lot of stuff for you and I'll list a few of the more important items. Camera, iron, cig case, pen, cig lighter, silver chain, 2 wings, misc. insig, 8 khaki shirts, 5 khaki pants, 1 trop worsted shirt, 1 battle jacket, short coat, blouse, 2 trop pants, hat, 4 oxfords, 1 green pants, 1 pink pants. Then the usual 19 socks, 19 ushirts, 11 drawers, 7 wool ushirts, etc. The only thing we didn't forward was extra soap, blades, cigarets, scotch, letters, and a couple of those dirty pictures. OK?. . .

The boys are all happy to hear that you're ok. When you go thru Fargo, be sure to look me up – after the war. Before, just call my honey – Louise is her name – and she's listed in the phone book as Mrs. E.R. Stern.

Lots of luck,
Ed Stern

(In reading Stern's letter, Glenn laughs at the memory of how all of the flyers would help themselves to the trunks left behind by downed crews. Watches, Air Corps-issue, were particularly in demand. Hank Zmudka had quite a collection, and no doubt hightailed it to Glenn's trunk on March 2 and helped himself to his pal's watch stash. "The navigators, in order to navigate celestially, were issued a very special little clock that was encased in a steel case. It was hung on springs so vibrations wouldn't affect its ability to keep time. They were very expensive, and I had a couple of those," Glenn says with a laugh. "I'd like to think that Hank was going for those and got them, before Davidow got there with Stern.")

May 22, 1945

I received a letter from Sgt. Childress' wife and Mrs. Slenker. They had heard the plane exploded in midair and that no one got out of the plane. But that has been proved wrong for Sgt. Childress is back and he knew more about what did happen than the other fellas in the formation. Did he say who the other fortunate one was? I want to know if it was my husband or not. I might as well receive it from someone other than the War Department. They are so blunt with it. Please, if you hear any further news, let me know. I do hope you have good news.

Mrs. Craig, Mrs. Waller, Mrs. Eckert, and Mrs. Slenker have all heard. Hope you share your good news.

Sincerely,
Mrs. Kenneth G. Tipton

May 22
Beaumont, TX

Dear Mrs. King
I was so glad for your letter saying that Glenn has been freed, and is all right. It must be a great relief for you to know that he is safe. The same day your letter came I had a V-mail from Glenn, written in France, which said he was well and was on his way home. Getting both letters at once was almost too much good news at one time – I fairly floated about from place to place!

Somehow, all along, I've had the feeling that Glenn was safe and unhurt, and that it would only be a matter of time before you had some word from him. I'm so happy for you. . . .

Sincerely,
Jean

———∞∞∞———

May 23, 1945

Dear Mrs. King,
I hope you have received good news too from your son.
I had a letter today from Kenneth – written May 1st – saying they were liberated two days before. He was well and had been all along. He didn't say who was with him.
I hope and pray they are home soon.
Mrs. Craig, Mrs. Waller, Mrs. Mang, Mrs. Eckert, Mrs. Slenker, Mrs. Childress and myself have all heard. I truly hope you share our good news.

Sincerely,
Mrs. Kenneth G. Tipton

(This is nearly a duplicate of the letter Mrs. Tipton sent the day before, written in desperation to learn any detail about the fate of her husband and his crew.)

———∞∞∞———

May 24, 1945 Telegram

> *WAR DEPARTMENT REPORTS JACK RETURNED*
> *TO MILITARY CONTROL MAY 1ST HAVE YOU HEARD*
> *ORALEE WALLER*

———

May 31, 1945
Signal Corps, United States Army

> *IN BEST OF HEALTH SAILING SOON WILL WIRE*
> *SOON AS I REACH THE STATES LOVE GLENN W. KING*
> *The inclosed* (sic) *message from a liberated prisoner of war was received from overseas via Army Communications facilities without cost to the sender. It is mailed herewith to the addressee designated in the message. In view of the contemplated immediate evacuation of all liberated prisoners to the United States, a reply to this message cannot be made.*

———

June 1, 1945

> *We were so glad to get your welcome letter yesterday bringing the blessed news of the safety of Glenn and that he will soon be home with you on leave. . . . It just seems to add a brighter outlook altogether. . . .We hope he arrives safely and this war will soon be over.*

> *Love,*
> *Mother* (Mary King)

———

99

June 5, 1945

> *Dear Mrs. King,*
>
> *So glad to know of your good news. I got your letters the same day I got my first letter from Kenneth. I have been up in the clouds ever since.*
>
> *I hope Glenn is home by now. I think Kenneth is on his way. He got his back hurt when he jumped. So did Edward Craig, the Co Pilot.*
>
> *Got a letter from Mrs. Waller today written Friday. She was going to meet Jack in a hour. He only got 13 days. She put that on the back of her letter.*
>
> *I heard from Kenneth that John Nostin was killed after bailing out. He didn't say how or what. Said he would tell me when he got home.*
>
> *I just thank God they are alive and will be home soon.*
>
> *Thanks for the lovely letters. They have helped me so much. If you're ever in Chattanooga, please look us up. I hope to meet you some time in the near future.*
>
> *Sincerely,*
> *Mrs. Tipton*

⸎

June 7, 1945
WASHINGTON DC

> *THE CHIEF OF STAFF OF THE ARMY DIRECTS ME TO INFORM YOU YOUR SON 2/LT GLENN W KING IS BEING RETURNED TO THE UNITED STATES WITHIN THE NEAR FUTURE AND WILL BE GIVEN*

AN OPPORTUNITY TO COMMUNICATE WITH YOU
UPON ARRIVAL.

JA ULIO
THE ADJUTANT GENERAL

———❦———

July 18, 1945
New Britain, Connecticut

> *Dear Mr. King,*
> *My folks have received sad news concerning their son,*
> *John. They received the official telegram on July 3rd.*
> *I am wondering if your son can possibly give my folks*
> *any details as to John's fate, such as if John spoke any last*
> *words, if he was wounded before he bailed out and where*
> *he rests. It would mean so much to my folks if they could*
> *hear from your son.*
>
> *Sincerely,*
> *Anna Nostin*

(Glenn doesn't believe that he wrote back to the Nostins because he had no information about the tailgunner who lost his life after bailing out of their burning airplane on March 2, 1945. John Nostin's name is inscribed on a war memorial in New Britain.)

CHAPTER SEVEN

BOX 51

By March 1945, all Midwest knew was that Glenn King was in a POW camp somewhere in Germany. Sgt. Childress' escape back to England had made it possible for the families to know that much at least. But anything could have happened since March 2.

Then a V-mail from Germany arrived and was tucked into Box 51, Midwest.

Glenn later learned that the postmistress promptly picked up the phone and dialed Leslie King at work. "There's some mail down here that I think you need to see immediately." That was all she would say.

Mr. King jumped into his '41 Oldsmobile and burned rubber to the post office. Seeing that familiar cursive across the face of the V-mail form was the first real confirmation Les King had that his boy was okay, "not even as much as a scratch," as Glenn phrased it.

If ever there were cause for rejoicing, tears of joy and one of Alice's angel food cakes, it was the day the Kings finally heard that Glenn was most definitely alive.

After that post-liberation week of misery in Moosburg, Glenn and hundreds of his fellow prisoners were trucked north to an airfield at Ingolstadt, a third of the way back to Nuremberg, along nearly the same path as their march to camp.

While the ex-POWs were waiting for a C-47 to carry them to France, a Stuka dive bomber circled and landed. "There was a rush of guys headed for it, but the MPs got to it first," Glenn says. "Two guys got out of the plane, Germans, who were surrendering because it was the end of the war.

"I stood there, ogling this plane, when someone yells 'King, hit the deck!' Our antiaircraft had been following the Stuka. As they rotated their guns around, I was going to be in the line of fire."

Glenn reacted with agility, flattening out and preparing for the worst, which did not come. Even though the war was all but over, Europe was still an extremely dangerous place. Without further incident, Glenn and the scores of other ex-POWs landed in Reims, France, ninety miles northeast of Paris and home to the Supreme Headquarters of the Allied Expeditionary Forces (SHAEF). The world remembers that on May 7, 1945, Germany signed the "Instrument of Surrender" in Reims. Glenn remembers it as the site of his first real shower since leaving England on March 2, 1945.

Because of the months of non-existent sanitation, every article of filthy clothing worn by the men – uniforms, flight suits, caps and boots – was piled onto huge columns and burned. German POWs were ordered to pick up the vermin-infested clothing and make sure the piles grew up rather than out, Glenn recalls.

Miraculously, the military had complete replacement uniforms at the ready for all the freed prisoners. "By then, they'd stopped building tanks," Glenn explains, "because they could see the end was coming. They needed to take care of their people."

The soldiers lived in Waldorf Astoria-like accommodations (tents) and got to eat whatever they wanted, which was a problem. After not eating for months, the former prisoners got sick. Sanitary facilities were slit trenches dug into the ground. But it was French ground, a sight better than German, and Glenn slowly began to regain his strength. He estimates that he weighed about 160 pounds, down from the 225 when he left the United States.

BOX 51

"I went through the chow line with my metal military issue tray. They had German POWs serving us. I saw some cling peaches and pointed. He put a half slice on my tray. I said, '*Mehr!*'" (Glenn had picked up more than a few words of German, in this case, the word for more.) The POW shook his head and said "*Nicht.*"

Glenn responded, "*Mehr,* you son of a bitch!" and was finally and most satisfyingly obliged with another peach half. In heavy syrup.

No one would ever again withhold food from Glenn King.

Glenn and all the former POWs were allowed to do whatever they wanted – eat, rest, write V-mail home and eat some more. He still has a few French francs clipped into the scrapbook his Mom kept, along with a solitary Reichsmark.

From Reims, the men headed to South Hampton, England, where they boarded the troopship Thomas Sumter, one of the many "Liberty" ships that transported POWs across the Atlantic to the United States. They couldn't leave until their escorts, small warships called Canadian Corvettes, showed up, Glenn says, because German U-boats were still trolling Europe's waters.

During the crossing the men talked of what was going to happen next. "We knew we wouldn't have to go back to Europe, but in the back of our minds was they'd need bombardiers to go back and bomb Japan. That was the greatest concern that I had."

Returning to war was worry for later. For now, there was glorious fried chicken to be had all the way back to New York. "The crew on the boat said they'd never seen such rough seas. The ocean was washing over the deck. All the infantry guys got sick. The Air Force guys would just go get another piece of chicken."

Nearly home, the men received word that the captain of the ship was very ill. Being a curious type, Glenn confesses that he went topside. "The ocean was pretty rough. These Corvettes all of a sudden were fairly close, and I could hear this 'plink! plink!' noise. It was like they were shooting at us. What I finally figured out was they were shooting a line over to our boat from the Corvette so they could transfer medicine for the captain. The plinking came from the sound the line made, bouncing off the ship. And I'm up there, just looking around, seeing what's going on. Not too smart! So I finally got out of there."

Sadly, the captain died of a heart attack, which cast a pall across the new shipmates. But the Navy steered the Thomas Sumter safely to Brooklyn, New York, per the yellowed newspaper clipping showing twenty-five Air Force guys, spiffed up in new uniforms, standing at attention on deck. Each man was headed to the western half of the United States – Big Fork, Montana; Salt Lake City; Denver; Payette, Idaho. "The Rocky Mountain people," Glenn points out.

Their next stop was Camp Kilmer in New Jersey. "There was what looked like a ferry boat as we went by the Statue of Liberty. There was a little band on top of it and girls and guys jumping up and down greeting us. Well, there were girls, mostly. They knew we were a Liberty Ship, coming home."

By evening, orders had been cut. Glenn called his folks to say he was on his way. "We were on a train that night heading for Denver."

He points out that the military used all its resources to speed the POWs home. "They'd even issued us money against our pay, so we had money in our pockets." That called for a steak dinner, so the next night, when Glenn got to Denver, he found a restaurant and dove into a New York strip.

He also called his folks again, this time to let them know he would be on a plane arriving in Casper.

The much-awaited, long-anticipated reunion nearly didn't take place.

"I left Denver and got as far as the airport in Cheyenne," Glenn explains. "While we were there waiting to re-board, they ran off a list of those who wouldn't be on this flight going to Casper because of the *overload condition* on the airplane. And I was one of those who wasn't going."

Remembering that day, Glenn is still furious. "Dammit, I know enough about flying that they can't be as accurate as that. My (now)

BOX 51

two-hundred pounds will not make any difference whether it's on the ground or in that aircraft.

"I went up to one of the flight attendants and told her my tale of woe. 'My parents are at the airport waiting for me now. What do I need to do to get an exception? I know a little bit about flying, and I ought to be able to make this flight!'

"She told me to go over and talk to the pilots, so I did. They didn't react much. But it wasn't too long before there was an announcement that Lt. King would be added to the list of those passengers going to Casper."

Thirty minutes had elapsed between the first and final announcement, plenty of time, unfortunately, for the Kings back in Casper to hear that Glenn had been bumped.

"Cheyenne was 175 miles from Casper. That wouldn't be too long of a haul for my Dad. When they got to the airport and got the word that I wouldn't be coming in on the plane until tomorrow because of excess loading, they decided, 'By golly, we're going to get him.'

"As they were driving in downtown Casper, the plane I should have been in flew overhead." The sight of the plane made them pause. "Wonder if there's a possibility he might be in that darned plane?

"So they turned around and went back to the airport. I was on the ground, waiting for them, and I saw this brown Oldsmobile whipping along at a good speed on the highway, heading for the airport. And I knew it was Mom and Dad and Jerry."

It had been more than a year since Glenn had seen his family.

Hitler's Luftwaffe, starvation, vermin, and Western Airlines had conspired – and failed – to prevent this reunion on the sidewalk outside the Casper airport. Glenn cannot describe it, other than to say it was a moment unlike any other in his life, filled with tears and hugs and more tears.

When everyone resumed breathing, Leslie King teased his son about not having the proper First Lieutenant's bars on his uniform. Glenn had been promoted while he was a prisoner. Later, Glenn would try to locate the proper insignia with no luck. So his Dad did what he always did – made a set with his own hands, honing the metal Monel into two precise First Lieutenant bars with clasps on the back. They are as shiny today as they were in 1945.

Of all the keepsakes from the war, it is the bars his Dad made that Glenn treasures most.

After arriving home, Glenn had several weeks to rest and gather his strength. The Casper paper ran the following:

Lt. Glenn King arrived home on June 16 and will spend a 60-day furlough with his parents, Mr. and Mrs. Leslie King, and brother, Gerry (sic), on Lewis street. Glenn was a bombardier on a B-17 with the Eighth Air Force in England. He was forced down over Germany March 2, and taken prisoner by the Germans. He was liberated from the 'Moosburg' prison camp on Sunday, April 29.

The Air Corps would add another 30 days to that furlough. By August 15, 1945, when the Japanese surrendered, Glenn officially was out of the bombing business. The Kings hosted a house party to celebrate his safe deliverance and the end of the war. Because liquor stores were ordered to close early that night, Glenn and his Dad drove to Edgerton, where the liquor stores had no intention of closing, to stock up on refreshments.

"All these people came, and had a drink, one after the other," Glenn recalls. "I finally found myself out in the backyard of our home, wandering around pretty much in a stupor. My Dad came out and took care of me."

While waiting for his official separation from the Air Corps, Glenn was invited to talk to the youth at the Community Church. Reverend Taylor had asked if he would be willing, and Glenn agreed. When he arrived on that summer evening, one hour before worship, he was surprised to read this in the program:

"Lieut. King will be present to answer questions that the young folks may wish to ask. Members of the Jr. Hi age group are especially invited to attend this meeting. In fact,

BOX 51

we make the invitation wider – anyone interested may attend. We regard these occasions when members of our armed forces speak as real opportunities for getting information and inspiration."

The horrors that Glenn had gone through the last few months of the war left him uneasy and unsure of how to begin. His three best pals from Midwest would not be coming home. And then there was Tripp. And Armbruster. And all the other guys lost in the skies over Europe.

"I didn't know what to say," he says simply.

The kindly minister told the reluctant lieutenant to "just tell the kids some of the places where you've been." And so Glenn began what would be a halting prelude to the talks he would give some fifty years later.

After Glenn returned home, one stop he was compelled to make was Midwest's branch of the Red Cross. The newspaper reported:

Lt. Glenn King who is home on furlough after being released from a German prison camp, recently was a visitor of the local Red Cross branch. He was very much interested in our Red Cross rooms, the way they were operated and enjoyed looking over the mail from the many boys and girls in the service elsewhere. He answered many questions asked him regarding the Germans and the European countries; he was most grateful for the help received from the Red Cross and especially the food packages received while being a prisoner. In appreciation, Glenn made a generous offering of $50 to the local branch of the Red Cross.

Glenn has written a check in support of the American Red Cross every year since graduating from college in 1950. If the Red Cross coat and boots saved his life, the food parcels sustained him. As for the tuna can that crossed the Atlantic in his coat pocket, it was only disposed of inadvertently, after his parents' house was sold following their deaths in the late 1970s.

It would have made a great show-and-tell for the junior high kids.

March 2, 1945: Part of Glenn's induction file from a German interrogation center, which accompanied him to Stalag XIIID, a POW camp in Nuremburg, and later to Stalag VIIa in Moosburg. After liberation, fellow soldiers stormed the office and managed to locate their personnel files. Glenn's has been held and viewed by hundreds of junior high students in Naperville, Illinois.

Glenn whittled this paddle from a scrap of wood he scrounged at the prison camp in Nuremberg. He used it to eat what little food was made available to the Allied airmen. By war's end, Glenn estimates, he weighed 160 pounds, down from 225 pounds.

CHAPTER EIGHT

COLORADO SCHOOL OF MINES

Throughout the war, Glenn had kept a correspondence with a young woman named Jean. They had gone to school together in Midwest until her father was transferred to the oilfields of Texas. Glenn had visited Jean while he was in bombardier training. Their relationship grew through the letters they had exchanged while Glenn was in the service. And while one might say there was an "understanding" between them, all told they had spent very little time together.

During Glenn's ninety-day leave following his return home, the Kings invited Jean to join them for horseback riding, fishing, and hiking in the Rockies. The setting could not have been more majestic or care-free, a well-earned and overdue respite from the war. Glenn was back on track to resume the life that his country had made him leave behind. At the age of twenty-one, Glenn proposed marriage and Jean accepted. With a pretty wife on his arm and a college degree in his future, he would restart the life he had set aside in 1943.

On Nov. 8, 1945, Glenn married Jean in Beaumont, Texas. On the way back to Midwest, they stopped at the School of Mines in Golden, Colorado, to pay a visit to the dean of engineering. Glenn thought that with his oil-field experience and with the contacts both sides of the family had in the industry, petroleum engineering made a lot of sense. Could he get into this school? You bet. The G.I. Bill would help make that possible.

So the dream deferred was within reach, but not quite like he had imagined.

School was tough, with twenty-one hours a semester of every conceivable type of chemistry, physics, chemical engineering and thermodynamics. Money was in short supply. Jean missed her parents. And both Glenn and Jean realized that neither knew the other beyond the uniform and the pretty face.

In less than a year, Jean returned to Texas to stay. The divorce eventually was finalized. He never heard from her again until nearly fifty years later, when an envelope arrived at his Naperville home with two photographs of Glenn, one of him standing with Jean at the Gulf of Mexico, near her home, and one of Glenn and Jerry on horseback in the Rockies. They are copies of the originals. No letter accompanied the photos, and there was no return address on the envelope.

In 1948, Leslie and Alice King moved to Rangely, Colorado, on a transfer with the oil company. Home from college on Christmas break, Glenn got a job roughnecking in the Rangely oil field. "I was broke. We were rigging up, getting ready to drill a hole and putting all the equipment together. I was working nights, the four to midnight shift, in a blinding snowstorm."

Glenn was being paid as the "floor man," doing whatever it took to get the well up and running from the ground. Another guy, "the derrick man," was paid more because he was on the girts, or the exterior supports of the derrick, connecting hoses to pipes in the snow and ice.

At one point, the derrick man struggled for more than an hour to connect a frozen hose, Glenn recalls. "So the boss man comes over to me and says, 'King! Do you think you can help him?'

"I don't climb derricks," Glenn replied, but did anyway. Because the ladder to access the outside of the well was useless, Glenn climbed the girts to assist the derrick man.

The two pulled and twisted, the hose too frozen to connect to the steel pipe. Glenn's gloves were wet with snow, and one hand slipped off the ice-covered metal. He managed to grab a girt with the other hand and spared himself a forty-foot drop to the ground. The hose was at last connected through their combined strength, and Glenn descended the rig with care.

That college degree grew better-looking every day. And he had another reason to stay in one piece: He'd met a girl a few months back.

When Glenn was just starting his summer coursework at the School of Mines, he decided to head to Denver to Elitch's Trocadero Ballroom ("where most of Denver danced and romanced," according to its online history.) He had heard that balladeer and bandleader Eddy Howard was playing. Ever the dancer, Glenn hoped to find a pretty girl and dance with her.

In a scene worthy of Rodgers and Hammerstein, Glenn looked across the crowded ballroom floor and "saw three good-looking girls. One was a blonde, two were brunette. So I headed for the blonde," Glenn recalls. "Someone got to her before I did, so I turned to that tall, good-looking brunette and asked her to dance." Dottie Gantert of Dubuque, Iowa, accepted the invitation of the tall stranger.

Dottie recently had moved to Denver on a whim. She'd left the Pentagon as a secretary to a colonel who led the first raid over Germany by the 95th Bomb Group. (He was not a gentleman, she would later inform Glenn.) After the war, she worked for Jackie Kennedy's stepfather, Hugh Auchinloss.

Deciding she had had enough of the civil service and the nation's capital, Dottie and a girlfriend brainstormed their options and decided to move to Denver because they had never seen mountains.

Dottie got a job working at Western Electric and happened to be at Elitch's on the same summer evening as Glenn because she, too, loved to dance. The slim, dark-haired beauty would share a dance with Glenn for the next sixty-three years. They married Sept. 3, 1949, at the home of Glenn's parents, just as his senior year was beginning.

When it came time to plan the wedding, Dottie and Glenn discussed the possibility of a service at the spectacularly situated Chapel of the Transfiguration in Grand Teton National Park. Although arranging a ceremony there grew a little too complicated, it would be a beloved destination for them through the years.

They honeymooned in Yellowstone National Park, where they would return for their 25th, 40th and 60th anniversaries. They always traveled west by car, and once they both had retired, at a leisurely pace.

Christmas 1949 found them back at Rangely in Glenn's 1933 Chevrolet. "Driving over those mountains, I knew I'd have to do work on it to get it back over the mountain to Golden," Glenn says. "That was typical of every place I took it," he says with a laugh.

At a company dance held in the Rangely Community Hall, several people approached Glenn to say that someone from Vernal, Utah, was looking for his Dad. This message was delivered a few times until Glenn began to worry. He saw his parents huddled in a corner of the hall. Something was definitely up.

Concerned, Glenn and Dottie approached his parents and heard his Dad ask, "How would you kids like to have a new car for Christmas?"

Mr. King had won a 1949 Chevrolet two-door sedan in a raffle. But because he had his eye on a 1950 Oldsmobile (and its 135-horsepower engine), he was happy to pass along the car to his son and new daughter-in-law. The '33 Chevy was duly sold, and Dottie and Glenn made it back over the Continental Divide in fine shape. There would be no need to tinker with this engine for some time.

It was common knowledge that the curriculum at the School of Mines was challenging, with the coursework for a bachelor's degree worthy of a master's. Still, Glenn persisted. "I had my goals. My father and mother, and I'll underline mother, wanted me to have a college education, and nothing else was going to get in the way."

Most of his fellow students were at "Mines" on the G.I. Bill. They didn't swap war stories, Glenn recalls, or if they did, he wasn't part of the conversation. "I had my eye on a different target. It was one that looked like that," he says, pointing to the sterling silver diploma that today hangs in his home office. "I couldn't get there quickly enough."

Glenn was named Outstanding Petroleum Engineer Graduate Class of 1950. His parents, brother Jerry and Dottie were there to watch him accept the award, which came with a twenty-five dollar stipend. "I was in total shock," Glenn recalls. "I had no idea that was coming."

The money went toward a pair of Ray Ban sunglasses. Glenn wore them for years – until they were accidently left behind at a gate at the Montreal Airport.

Because Glenn had mowed the lawns of the big bosses at Midwest and roustabouted and roughnecked there his entire life, "I really wanted to prove myself outside the contacts of Midwest."

So Glenn and Dottie moved to Powell, Wyoming, where Glenn worked as a roustabout in the oil fields until a full-time engineering job opened up with Amoco, where he had interned on and off during school breaks. "Right after the war, the oil industry had been so short of engineers that with the new crop of college graduates, they had over hired," Glenn says.

The Kings were in Powell about six months until an engineering job became available in Levelland, a west-Texas field operation where sandstorms are common. But having done just about every nasty job in an oil field since he was a kid, he was not undone by the wind and grit.

A promotion and transfer to Tulsa, Oklahoma, followed. It was all office sitting and no field work or climbing. But it was a tremendous opportunity to learn. Glenn was the liaison between production and research.

"The only reason I was qualified was because of all of this background that I had had in my life doing things in oil fields. I ended up working very closely with research. This was at the time that Amoco invented hydraulic fracturing. I ended up working directly with the two fellows who are credited with its discovery, George Howard and Bob Fast," Glenn says.

Glenn was about to contribute to the company's bottom line in a significant way.

First, a lesson in hydraulic fracturing, or fracking: Sand is mixed with water that is then pumped into the earth to dislodge oil and natural gas. At the time, about a half pound or less was used per gallon of injected fluids into the earth. When the company was testing this process, Halliburton, the service company it used, charged Amoco four cents a pound for sand.

In a report that landed on Glenn's desk, a field superintendent recommended using screened river sand instead of the huge volumes of the preferred (and expensive) Flint Shot Ottawa Sand 20/40 mesh. (The name still draws a chuckle from Glenn.) "Sand is sand," Glenn recalls thinking. "What did I know about sand? Nothing. If I wanted sand, I'd go to a lumberyard. So I looked in the phone directory and called a lumberyard. They'd sell the exact sand to us for one and a quarter cents per pound in hundred-pound bags. As soon as I hung up, I dashed to my boss, who dashed to his boss."

Glenn's father was fracking wells in northwest Colorado. "He had a double-stall garage filled with Flint Shot sand," Glenn says. "When we showed the company that we could use the stuff bought directly from lumberyards and store it in garages like my father, Halliburton dropped the price of their sand. It saved us millions of dollars."

Seven years after Glenn had landed in a tree in Germany, he and Dottie were blessed with their first son, Larry, on August 16, 1952, in Tulsa. Having a child changes everything, of course, particularly so in the face of war. The Korean Conflict, as it was known, was raging a world away when an Air Force colonel interviewed reservist 1st Lt. Glenn King to determine his availability.

"When I had separated from the service in Santa Monica, I took the option of going into the Reserve so if I were called back, I could continue to wear lieutenant bars on my shoulder," he explains. "But I had no plan to stay in for any time at all.

"When this colonel came around and asked if I were available to go back into the service, I said not as a flyer. His comment was, 'If you won't return as a flyer, we will totally have to retrain you.'

Under his breath, Glenn said, "So be it."

Shortly after this encounter, Glenn officially was separated from the Air Force Reserve. He was twenty-nine years old.

The next stop on the corporate highway was Fort Worth, Texas, where Glenn was made a reservoir engineer, the guy who determines how much oil will ultimately be pumped out of the ground. The city would become precious to Glenn and Dottie for it is where their second son, Steve, was born on August 2, 1954.

The following year, the Kings packed up the '49 Chevrolet and moved to what would be Glenn's favorite post: Sweetwater, Texas. "I was in high cotton! I loved the job. I was field engineer, with a staff of young engineers and doing everything that needed to be done to make an oil field successful."

The College of Mines had taught its students "ruthless accuracy" when it came to surveying new wells, and that meant accommodating for hills, valleys and even the undulations of sage brush. Glenn taught a generation of young engineers how to use a magnifying glass to read the numbers on a Vernier scale on a transit to ensure wells would be drilled on property owned by the company. An oil well drilled on the wrong piece of land meant a lawsuit, delays, cost overruns and headaches aplenty.

Odessa, Texas, came two years later, with double the field staff and much the same work. The Kings bought a house there just in time to be transferred back to Fort Worth, where Glenn was put in charge of the Proration Department. "I hated it!" he says of the job that required him to testify before the railroad commission – the regulatory agency for the oil industry – trying to get permission to drill and produce wells. These meetings were so highly charged and so important to the company that

Glenn, if necessary, had *carte blanche* to approve and move ahead with multi-million dollar projects.

The pressure, he says, was unrelenting, so it made those occasional road trips to Colorado to visit his parents and Jerry all the sweeter. His young boys particularly got a kick out of visiting where the deer and the antelope truly do play.

Of particular interest to Larry and Steve was a real mountain lion that had been treed and stuffed in the early 1950s. Grandpa King had shot it while on a horseback guided trip in the mountains. It was prominently displayed in the Kings' living room.

All of the Kings, with the exception of Alice, had hunted game all their lives. Elk and pheasant meat were favorites. The mountain lion, however, was strictly for sport.

"When our boys were the likes of six and four, we had to watch them to make sure they didn't break off the whiskers," Glenn says with a laugh.

Through the years, the pelt disintegrated. "Mother wanted to get rid of it," Glenn recalls. "My nephew Greg, who loved hunting, said he'd love to have the head." So Leslie King's mountain lion head today stands guard in Richardson, Texas. Its whiskers are still intact.

Amoco continued to promote Glenn throughout the south, the last stop being New Orleans. The Kings built their second house there and Glenn added off-shore drilling to his resume. He taught Dottie how to shoot skeet and bought her "a real fancy shotgun." They lived there for thirteen years. Despite their many moves, both Larry and Steve considered New Orleans home. Larry graduated from LSU and worked in finance. Steve, two years younger, followed right behind his brother at LSU.

In 1975, Glenn greeted Dottie on the driveway of their home with a huge smile and a celebratory martini. They were being transferred to Chicago so Glenn could be in charge of an Amoco engineering group.

He was at the top of the oil game. The view looked pretty darned good, even if there weren't any mountains.

Glenn held several other positions at Amoco until his retirement in 1984. His most gratifying role, he says, was leading a group of engineers dubbed the Green Light Boys. "I've never worked with a group that had such a capacity for work," he recalls. They had three to four years' experience out of school. "You'd just put the problem in front of them and get out of the way," he says with a laugh.

His last post, manager of NGL Coordination (Natural Gas Liquids), put him at the pinnacle of his oil career. He watched over the bottom line for the royalty owners, trying to get fair market value for the by-products generated by oil and gas production. Special projects came up for him to coordinate, such as a new pipeline in the Gulf of Mexico, which constituted millions of dollars of revenue for the company and carried huge responsibilities. When the pressure became intense, his philosophy was, "Take two aspirin and get down to solving the problem."

Not too shabby for a roustabout and roughneck from Wyoming.

When Glenn retired from Amoco, just before it was purchased by British Petroleum (BP), he was fêted at a luncheon and presented with a book filled with hundreds of letters and well-wishes from every office in every department in every city where he had worked. They are bound in a book three inches thick. The details contained in those letters reflect the kind of man Glenn is: thoughtful, hardworking, ethical, attentive to detail, a great guy. Everyone had something to say and everyone said it well:

You can be mighty proud of how you have managed and coordinated our plant liquids business. . . .

I will miss your contributions and positive approach . . . .

Your hard work and dedication have been greatly appreciated. . . .

I'll never forget a story you told me once of hanging in a tree looking down the muzzle of several German machine guns, thinking that if you survived that mess you'd never again feel bad about hard times at home or at the office. That's been inspirational to me. I'm glad I've known you.

Late Fall 1945: Glenn at home in Midwest, Wyoming.

Sept. 3, 1949: wedding day for Dottie and Glenn at his parents' home in Rangely, Colorado. After a honeymoon in Yellowstone National Park, the couple lived in Golden, where Glenn finished his senior year at the Colorado School of Mines. The Kings were married for sixty-three years.

Leslie King, Glenn's father, with a mountain lion he shot during a hunting trip in the Rockies. The car is a 1950 Oldsmobile.

Larry and Steve, Glenn and Dottie's sons, circa 1959, in Sweetwater, Texas.

CHAPTER NINE

"SOME THINGS YOU NEVER FORGET"

There was nothing retiring about Glenn's retirement from Amoco in 1984.

The day after his last in the Chicago office, he put on a necktie and headed to his new job as a consultant for Harris Bank. He traveled on its behalf to Tulsa, Denver, New Orleans and Houston. "It was a great thing for me, and helped take care of the wind-down," he says.

When the bank consultancy job ended in 1987, Glenn answered a newspaper advertisement from the Better Business Bureau, which was looking to train volunteer arbitrators for automotive disputes in the Chicago area. It was a perfect job for this keen listener, fair thinker and lifelong car guy.

"My whole career was problem solving. When you get two parties laying out arguments that support what they think is right versus what the other guy thinks is right, you problem-solve the dispute."

He has kept a binder filled with the more than two hundred cases he ultimately arbitrated for the BBB. The work was hugely satisfying. In fact, he was honored as Arbitrator of the Year in 1992.

After he had been settling cases for six or seven years, "the hierarchy in the BBB decided they should only have attorneys hearing these cases," Glenn says, "so they were no longer needing engineers, in spite of the fact the majority of the hearings involved automobiles."

While he missed the complexities of the cases and the resolutions (almost always in favor of the manufacturer), Glenn had become active in Community Radio Watch, a group of citizen volunteers who helped police prevent crime by patrolling the community.

"One of the main missions was to drive around Naperville and look for open garage doors," Glenn explains. "We'd write down the address, and send out a letter over the police chief's autograph, cautioning home-owners to keep their garage doors closed. We'd send out 2,500 letters a year."

Crime got a little more real the day Glenn, with Dottie by his side, pulled out of their driveway and spotted a car that had been identified as "suspect" in a string of house robberies. Car man that he was, Glenn remembered "Caddy with a bustle-back trunk" without looking at his notes. There it was, parked on his very street.

Glenn and Dottie watched a man with a stocking cap pulled low over his face walk down a nearby driveway and head toward the Cadillac. "We were restricted to get the license plate only," Glenn explains. "And there was no license plate! But there was a frame there with the name of a Ford dealership."

They followed the car at a discreet distance across town. At the time, Glenn carried one of those newfangled car phones in a bag, so Dottie called the police while they kept an eye on the Cadillac. The police eventually were able to deduce the buyer of the car from Glenn's information and arrested him a week or so later. Because of his involvement in the case, Glenn got to see the "loot" the man had accumulated during his spree. It took more than fifty paper bags to hold it all.

Glenn would have kept driving around checking for open garages had cataracts not gotten in the way of reading the house numbers.

So he left patrolling and took a seat on the board of directors of Naperville Crime Stoppers, serving for twenty-seven years. He stepped down in January 2014, one month shy of his ninetieth birthday.

In 1994, Glenn received a call from Linda Rose, a friend from Knox Presbyterian Church who was a teacher at Jefferson Junior High School. The eighth graders were studying the Second World War. Would Glenn be interested in coming to talk to the kids as part of the World War II Speakers Program?

Other than kidding with Dottie about cling peaches and mentioning the tuna can to his sons once or twice, Glenn never really had talked about the war. He explains: "You had a story, but everyone else had one, too. Just an aside: out of my class, I was the only one who received commissioned-officer status. The others were sergeants or corporals and so forth. I think as a result, I didn't want to spread around how 'great' Glenn King was."

But the war had been nearly fifty years ago. Amoco had trained him to speak in public, so his presentation skills had sharpened quite a bit since that summer's night in front of the youth group at Community Church in Midwest. Motivating him, too, was the knowledge that he had an opportunity to let the next generation "know what the war was all about."

He remembers digging up his wood paddle, the silverware that was "liberated" from the guards at the POW camp and his papers from the interrogation center with an enraged 21-year-old bombardier's picture pasted to the front. He jotted a few notes. Dottie encouraged a bit of restraint regarding bombing targets. He had a model of a B-17. It was imperfect because no escape hatch was scribed on the underside, but it would help illustrate his story to the kids.

He spoke to his first class that year and continued to do so until 2008, a fulfilling and meaningful connection that he has treasured. His reward, he says, was seeing a room full of kids perched on the edges of their seats as he recounted the missions he had flown, and how a parachute had saved his life. The kids could see and touch the tangibles of his life in wartime – the pen and pencil set from Fran, the wood paddle, the medals, his POW papers.

At the end of one presentation, a student asked, "How do you remember all that stuff?"

Glenn told him, "Some things you never forget."

Every so often, Glenn would be out and about in Naperville and be recognized. "A child would come and say, 'Are you Mr. King who came up and talked to us at Jefferson Junior High?' It happened a few times. It felt good. And I liked hearing what their grandfathers did in the war."

At the behest of the mother of a girl who had missed his talk one year at Jefferson, Glenn brought the story directly to their home. Glenn sat at the dining room table and related some of the stories that he had told her classmates. At the end, he presented her with a pair of bombardier wings. She was enchanted, he recalls.

Sadly, two years later the child died, and her mother asked Glenn if he wanted the wings back. They were hers to keep, he assured her. It had been his honor to share his story with her daughter.

When the school canceled the speakers program in 2009, Glenn was invited one last time – to record his story on a DVD that would be used yearly during the WWII unit. Glenn declined. He wrote to the junior high:

> *Based on the student and staff reaction to my presentation, I have always been convinced that this was a very worthwhile effort. The individual students' written notes to me are priceless. They reveal an understanding of what happens in 'war' that they knew little or nothing about. As you might recall, my presentation reveals my flying combat while bombing Germany and then becoming a P.O.W. I cannot comprehend that 'scheduling constraints' would preclude your students from having such an experience. . . . My presentation requires eye-to-eye contact with the students and their responses. They end up sitting on the edge of their chairs as I tell them of my war experiences.*

Over the years, Glenn received scores of thank you notes from the kids. He has saved a few, this one being a particular favorite of Dottie's:

Hello Mr. King!

I loovvedd your presentation! It was the funniest! I especially liked the part when you were going out of the jet into the parachute, it really made my day! I was deeply honored to see you, you really made this experience complete. By the way (of all the speakers), you were my favourite! Thank you so much for coming to Jefferson. It made me experience what it was like to be a soldier in WWII. Who needs Superman when we got you to save the day?

With all my heart,

Mary

On the cover of the card is a picture of the Man of Steel, with these words: *Mr. Glenn King! The Super Man of Our Time.*

Although he had declined Jefferson's invitation, Glenn did record his stories of wartime. Another sixth grade class in Naperville videotaped one of his presentations. And in 2005, Hines Veterans Hospital in Chicago invited all former POWs to record oral histories as part of the POW Living History Project. Glenn's story of how he was shot down and imprisoned in Germany is recorded on a DVD and is part of a permanent video record in the Library of Congress.[5]

In the 1990s, Glenn was evaluated at Hines for Post-Traumatic Stress Disorder. Known as Soldier's Heart after the Civil War and Shell Shock in the Great War, PTSD was of great interest to Hines in trying to reach out to veterans coming back from Iraq. As part of that program, Glenn was evaluated. As Dottie could have told them, he had it. Every time Glenn had dozed off in his recliner and Dottie lightly touched his arm, "I'd jump about a foot. My whole body would react," Glenn says. Loud noises still affect him. Movies with scenes of planes exploding are unwatchable.

---

5 Glenn's interview in the Library of Congress is hosted at http://lcweb2.loc.gov/diglib/vhp/bib/39378

While Hines helped him to understand the cause and nature of these reactions, Glenn declined any intervention. "They felt I was coping well," he says. More importantly, he adds, "I thought I was coping well." Telling his story of survival to the junior high kids may very well have helped him to "settle down" in his mind what needed settling, to use his expression.

Glenn has remained a trim one-hundred eighty-five pounds through the years. He doesn't get particularly hungry, he says, and knows it is a consequence of his time in the camps. What definitely was a response to his being a prisoner became apparent in France, when he started to scan the ground for plants – or anything – to eat. When he was back in Midwest and doing the same thing, he realized this habit borne of starvation needed to be broken. Like everything else he set his mind to, he did.

Glenn and Dottie endured the loss of their firstborn, Larry, to stomach cancer in 1981. He was twenty-nine years old, married to Pam and father to one-month-old Lisa. He had graduated from LSU and was enjoying a meteoric rise in the banking industry.

Dottie made it to his side in time to say good bye. Glenn was held up during a business trip to southwest Wyoming, unable to get a flight to New Orleans.

In time, Pam King remarried. Lisa became big sister to Karen in 1985. Glenn and Dottie's first great-grandchild, Connor, was born to Lisa in 2008.

In memory of their son, the Kings underwrote the acquisition of a bell for Naperville's Millennium Carillon Tower. A bronze plaque next to the tower base on Naperville's Riverwalk is embossed with *Glenn and Dorothy King* and the outline of a bell. The molded brass G-sharp bell is inscribed with the following:

> *In Memory*
> *Larry M. King*
> *1952-81*
> *Glenn King Family*

Glenn was at the event known as the Raising of the Bells. He brought his battered hard hat from oil field days and placed it on top of the bell so he could photograph its scale. Every once in a while, when he is goes up into the Carillon tower, he wanders past Larry's bell and quietly gives it a pat.

At one time or another, all the King men have worked as either a roustabout (general oil field work) or a roughneck (literally on the rig). Steve King, on a break from LSU, had the distinction of working on an offshore drilling rig. Drilling work is exponentially more dangerous on a platform bobbing in the sea. The job was arranged by Glenn. "He probably thought I was trying to kill him," Glenn says.

Well into the assignment, Steve was asked to carry two large pails of lubricant up a set of stairs from a platform to the one above it. The pails contained lead and each weighed about one hundred pounds.

Observing the platforms rocking in the water, Steve pointed out to the boss that there was a perfectly serviceable crane available to do the job. The boss replied, "Take it up, or I'll call a boat (to take you to shore)." Steve told him he'd best call the boat.

"While he was out there," Glenn says, "he saw these fifty-year-old guys doing the same things he was doing. He knew he didn't want to be doing that when he was fifty. It shaped him up pretty fast."

Turns out the safety record of this outfit was not the best. Glenn did what he could to let the right people know about that, and Steve turned his efforts to construction, ultimately graduating from LSU and building houses across the south. He now owns his own development company and continues as a successful homebuilder in Plano, Texas, where he lives with wife, Beth. They have three children. Jennifer, the oldest, is a teacher. Christine, a civil engineer, and Parker, a college junior, are following in their Dad's construction footsteps.

Glenn's brother, Jerry, twelve years younger than Glenn, graduated from the University of Denver with a degree in Business and worked for Johnson and Johnson. He has four sons: Greg, Chris, Kevin and Darren. He now lives in Elizabethtown, Kentucky, where he is cared for by his wife, Meta, a native of Germany.

Jerry has valiantly battled Parkinson's disease for the past seven years, so the brothers mostly visit by phone. Recently, however, Steve and Greg gathered Glenn in Naperville for a road trip to visit Jerry. Photographs were taken and stories exchanged. Chris came from California to meet up with everyone and published a full-color keepsake book documenting the visit. Glenn keeps it on his coffee table.

Getting together with family over the years has been important to Glenn, particularly if hunting was involved. Steve tried many times to win his dad on the notion of a pheasant-hunting trip to southwestern Kansas outside the tiny town of Sublette. With retirement and "all the time in the world," Glenn decided this might be the perfect adventure for everyone to "jump start" the hunting tradition that he had known with his father. "I loved to go with my Dad hunting," Glenn recalls. And while Leslie King had hunted in order to put food on his family's table, this generation of Kings would be doing it mostly for sport.

The first day of the hunt, Glenn and Dottie agreed, would be on their nickel. After a full weekend, they were sure that everyone would be as captivated by hunting as Glenn had always been. And sure enough, the Sublette adventure has become a tradition lasting more than twenty years. Marksmen abound in the family.

In 2005, a serious car accident just outside of Sublette totaled Glenn's Trailblazer. He wasn't feeling so hot either. Even though "every step hurt," he stayed in the hunt and shot his limit. The following year was his last as a pheasant hunter.

These days, Glenn is content to look at a framed photograph of his family taken on the fields of Sublette. It hangs just below a wall hanging made of Ring-necked pheasant feathers. Above everything is a 12-gauge muzzle-loading shotgun purchased in 1858 by his great-grandfather. It was last used in 1907 to hunt prairie chickens on the North Dakota prairie.

Glenn and Dottie underwrote the purchase of a bell for Naperville's Millennium Carillon in memory of their son Larry, who died in 1981. Glenn's hard hat rests atop the bell prior to its installation in order to show its scale.

1982: Glenn and Dottie King in Naperville, Illinois.

One of the scores of thank-you notes Glenn has received from students
in the Naperville School District after recounting his story of being shot out
of the skies over Germany. This note was one of Dottie King's favorites.

CHAPTER TEN
DOTTIE

When real retirement settled in, the Kings decided a road trip to air out their new Cadillac was just the ticket to celebrate their 60th anniversary in 2009. To Glenn's way of thinking, a 4,300-mile driving vacation is nothing short of perfect, particularly with his beloved Dottie by his side and mountains looming in the distance.

Glenn always had wanted to see Sun Valley, Idaho. (As a child skiing in Wyoming, Glenn had to walk back up any hill he skied down. If you were to believe the movies, there were things called ski lifts to take you back up. He wanted to see that most of all, he says with a laugh.)

The Kings cruised into Golden, Colorado, and revisited the School of Mines, then wound their way to Jackson, Wyoming, after stopping at the Vernal, Utah, cemetery where Leslie and Alice King are buried.

It was a sweet and slow trek, with plenty of time to reflect on the multiple blessings in their lives. Glenn's parents once had arranged for a pair of ponies at their home in Rangely so Steve and Larry could be proper cowboys for the weekend. The boys, under the watchful eye of a local wrangler, actually trotted into town, tied up in front of the drugstore, and sauntered in for a malt.

The outdoors would continue to play a large role in the lives of the Kings. Both boys would become Eagle Scouts, with their Dad serving as assistant Scoutmaster and their Mom the determined merit-badge shepherd. "We all cherished our Friday nights," Steve King recalls, for the joy of being together.

When Glenn and Dottie weren't on a tour bus to the Canadian Rockies or sailing a fjord in Alaska, they were reveling in the gift of grandparenthood. After raising two boys (and all the shenanigans that implies), Dottie especially was taken with her granddaughters. Beth recalls that when Jennifer and Christine were at the perfect age for tea parties, Dottie would wear dress-up finery and sip "tea" with them all afternoon. It was clear there was no other place Dottie would rather be than in that moment with her girls.

The Kings returned home from their anniversary road trip after three weeks, having lost track of time on the road west. Dottie was a longtime volunteer at the Serendipity Resale Shop, a downtown Naperville thrift store operated to benefit Little Friends, Inc., which serves adults and children with developmental disabilities. Glenn says Dottie loved her time at the shop, which is run entirely by volunteers. Hers was an affirming and long-time affiliation that had her sorting through donations, looking for treasures amidst the piles of what-not and pricing them a little higher than the rest in order to further the ends of this worthy cause.

When her health began to fail in 2010, it was her great regret that she could no longer spend her Mondays at Serendipity. The president/CEO of Little Friends sent a letter thanking her for her thirty-plus years' assistance. Today, it hangs on Glenn's office wall.

Dottie's assistance was invaluable to Glenn, too, supporting him in his school talks. It was she who kept a light touch on the tiller of his stories, suggesting he bear in mind the age of his audience and describe how he had bombed bridges and ball bearing factories, rather than towns or rail yards.

She had accompanied Glenn to Chicago to meet up with Mr. and Mrs. Hank Zmudka in the early 1950s, staying behind in the apartment with Hank's wife and two children while Glenn and his wartime co-pilot headed to the corner tavern. (It was there that Glenn learned he had flown with Tipton because Davidow, the assigned bombardier, didn't get out of bed. Or something to that effect.) They talked mostly of their new lives as engineers. Other than that, Glenn and Hank didn't really have much to talk about.

In 1965, while they were living in New Orleans, Glenn and Dottie entertained Bob Poage and his wife for a weekend. The reunion had gone well with his old navigator, but as with Hank, theirs was a connection forged in wartime. Twenty years later, it was good to catch up over a meal and savor the peace they had all sacrificed so much for. Beyond Christmas cards, Glenn would not hear any more from the Starkel crew.

One early morning in February 2012, Dottie suffered a cerebral hemorrhage. She called out to Glenn, who came running to her side and cradled her in his arms. He called 911 and directed the first responders to break down the door of their home because he refused to let go of Dottie. Once at the hospital, she was able to squeeze Glenn's hand up until ten o'clock that morning. The next day, February 19, she was gone.

At her memorial service at Knox Presbyterian Church, Greg King shared his remembrances of Aunt Dottie, selecting the wisdom of Proverbs: *She stretches out her hand to the poor; yea, she reaches forth her hands to the needy; Her children arise up, and call her blessed; her husband also, and he praises her.*

When preparing for the service, Glenn was asked what music he would like to have played. He cast about for something that would mean the most to the both of them. *Great Is Thy Faithfulness* is a soaring and comforting hymn, as is *I to the Hills Will Lift My Eyes*. These definitely would be sung during the service. But what really would be sweet was Francis Craig's song *Near You*. It had been a big hit for the Andrews Sisters in 1947. Glenn and Dottie had always considered it *their* song:

> *There's just one place for me, near you*
> *It's like heaven to be, near you*
> *Times when we're apart*
> *I can't face my heart*

Say you'll never stray
More than just two lips away.

If my hours could be spent, near you
I'd be more than content, near you
Make my life worthwhile
By telling me that I'll
Spend the rest of my days, near you.

The love song captured Glenn and Dottie perfectly.

Since Dottie's death, Glenn slowly has resumed his life in the community. He attends church, plays bridge, enjoys the symphony and occasionally speaks to groups – including the 8th Air Force Historical Society in Chicago – about his wartime experiences.

His neighborhood book club invited him to speak on Laura Hillenbrand's *Unbroken*, the mesmerizing biography of Louis Zamperini, who suffered terribly at the hands of his Japanese captors during World War II. People frequently ask Glenn how the Germans treated him during his captivity: "I tell them that they didn't feed us very well," he says. "In fact, they didn't feed us hardly at all, but there was no physical abuse that I experienced."

Glenn follows up with the story of his first day at the interrogation center, when he persuaded the German guard to return the watch given to the American sergeant by his parents. He talks about the guards who herded him and his fellow captives below the Frankfort train platform and away from the increasingly hostile workmen. And he recalls the first "meal" the guards handed to him and co-pilot Ed Craig the day they parachuted into Germany.

Glenn's was a terrible ordeal, but one with a few streaks of light and kindness, something he pays forward every time he stands before a room full of eager listeners. And he knows he could not have done it without Dottie, who loved, protected and supported him enough so he could start telling his stories about the war. She made it possible for him to not only piece back his life but to strive and succeed as a student and, later, as a corporate executive. Dottie tended the hearth fires, loving and caring for their boys while Glenn was getting his arms around the next promotion. Theirs was a mutual and rare loving partnership, one that lasted sixty-three years.

Dottie knew about Glenn's first marriage. It had meant so little to Glenn that it mattered not at all to her. Glenn thought he had pitched most of the memories related to it years ago. Once this book was started, however, a few things pertaining to Jean filtered to the top – a newspaper clipping here, a photo there, and a couple of letters. (Regrettably, in a burst of clean-up fever, Glenn had thrown away the letters that he had written to his parents during the war. One imagines Alice King would not have approved.)

Dottie, on the other hand, had carefully amassed the many bits and pieces of the King archive through their multiple moves, gathering them into an antique camelback trunk that had belonged to her family. And while Glenn's letters were a loss, what Dottie kept has illuminated her husband's story.

"I never knew anyone who could love me as deeply as Dottie loved me," Glenn says. "I knew it early, and I knew it at the very end."

CHAPTER ELEVEN

WE REMEMBER

When they came home from the war, most World War II veterans, including Glenn, chose not to speak about their experiences. Glenn says he felt that compared to what happened to his high school friend Johnny Sinadin and the other guys who suffered on Japan's notorious Hell Ships, "Why would I talk about the fact that I had a little tough time in Germany?"

It took decades for many of the stories horror and otherwise – to be told. Likewise, it took nearly sixty years before a World War II memorial was built to honor the American men and women who had served in the Armed Forces.

In 2008, Honor Flight Chicago was created to provide an all-expenses-paid trip for area veterans to see the memorial built in their honor in Washington, D.C. It took a few years for Glenn to decide to accept HFC's offer, but after the visit, he called it "one of the most memorable days of my life."

In preparation for the flight, Glenn rummaged around and found a leather A2 bomber jacket facsimile (the original was incinerated when his plane went down), and pinned on his bombardier wings and the 8th Air Force patch. He hoped to run into someone he knew.

Chicago television reporter Corey McPherrin was covering the flight in preparation for a story titled "Fox Chicago Travels with Honor Flight Chicago." McPherrin's father, a veteran, died before he could be an Honor Flight participant, so it was an emotional trip for the reporter, Glenn, and the many veterans (plus volunteer escorts) who filled the plane.

Glenn says he was deeply moved by the memorial. The Freedom Wall on the west side of the National Mall features row upon row of gold stars in relief, each representing 100 American military deaths. In all, there are 4,048 stars. The inscription at the base of the wall reads: *Here We Mark the Price of Freedom.* "That got to me," he says.

In the Atlantic Pavilion, each state has its own granite pillar and bronze wreath. Seeing Wyoming – strength and sadness made manifest – rising up on the Memorial Plaza was overwhelming, he says. He thought back to the faces in uniform that filled Midwest's drug store window all those years ago. He was making this trip for them, and for the guys who didn't make it back to Great Ashfield.

Glenn didn't run into anyone from the 385th, which probably was just as well. No one on the trip did much talking because there was so much to take in, too much to remember. Glenn sat on a bench near the memorial and was approached by McPherrin and asked of his impressions of the memorial and to speak about his service during the war. Glenn's recollections, particularly of how he had lost his three best friends, became part of the broadcast that aired on Veteran's Day 2010.

After an exhausting day touring the Capitol, the Honor Flight guests returned to Chicago. Glenn looked out the plane window "and there were all these fire trucks. I thought something was wrong. It wasn't too long before the water started to hit the plane. They were watering us down in welcome as we came up to the gate.

"I was in the back of the plane – they loaded the most capable guys first and wheelchairs last. I kept hearing this noise – loud clapping and cheering – as we slowly left the plane. There was a huge line of people to greet us in the airport, shaking our hands and thanking us. It was just beautiful."

When he got home, Glenn carried unopened a large brown envelope marked with his name. During "mail call" on the flight home, he learned that family members – as well as complete strangers – had written to the veterans to thank them for their service. Glenn waited a day before sitting down to read the dozens of letters sent his way.

Dear Granddad,

I hope you had a good day with all the other veterans visiting the museums and memorials. I think it's really cool to have a veteran of WWII as a granddad and be able to experience all of your interesting stories first hand.

I can't thank you enough for your contributions to our country. I hope you had a great day.

Love,
Parker

Dear Glenn,

I OFTEN try to imagine how different our lives and the world would be today if it wasn't for the sacrifices that were made and the lives that were given by what truly is THE Greatest Generation our nation has ever seen. We would not have the freedom and the liberty that we enjoy so very much everyday if it were not for what you and all of our WWII veterans had done for us and for past and future generations. I find myself tearing up when I think about the sacrifices that were made. But they're not so much tears of sadness, but tears of joy, honor and gratitude for the quality of life that has been given to all of us by you and our veterans.

I truly thank you for this gift and it will NEVER be forgotten or taken for granted.

Love,
Kevin and Diane (Glenn's nephew and wife)

Dear Dad,

I guess you're on your way back to Chicago as you read this. Tracey with Honor Flight called a couple of days ago and explained more to me about what your trip was all about. Sounds like you had an incredible day. Hope you had the chance to meet and compare experiences with other servicemen.

As you know, I've heard most of the stories over the years but they seem to have more impact as time goes by. Especially in these times when so many people seem to take this country for granted, it becomes more evident how spectacular the efforts of an entire generation were in defending our country and its way of life. When we talk about it here with the kids and relate that you said others were basically Christine's age (Steve's daughter, Glenn's granddaughter), *it really drives home how inspiring the achievements were.*

Hopefully all of this is not lost on today's young people. You should be very proud to have done your part in communicating all of those the 7th grade classes over the years. I know you've had a great day. What an honor! I look forward to hearing about it.

Love,
Steve

———— ⬥ ————

Dear Glenn,
...I would like to express my heartfelt admiration and appreciation for your courage and all you went through.

I know for many, many years you didn't want to talk about your wartime experiences. I can only imagine how being a POW affected your life. I am so grateful that you have been able to share your stories with all of your family and so many others. We have all learned so much from you. ...

I want to thank you for being a wonderful father-in-law, grandfather, and most of all, a wonderful dad to Steve. I know having you as his role model helped mold him into the kind, inspiring, and loving father and husband that he is – just like you.

I love you and Dottie so very much.

Beth (Glenn's daughter-in-law)

———— ⬥ ————

Hey Grandad,
I hope you are having a nice time visiting all the museums and memorials that are such a huge part of your life. I am sure your visit is stirring up plenty of memories and emotions from when you served in the war. I want you to know that I truly appreciate the sacrifices you made

for our freedom and our country. I can't begin to imagine what it was like for you out there fighting for us. However, I know through your experiences, you learned about courage, service, and sacrifice.

You have truly made being a World War II veteran part of your life. I am so lucky to hear your stories firsthand. I can't wait until Connor is old enough to listen to your stories and understand what a remarkable Great-Granddad he has.

Thank you!

Love,
Lisa

Dear Granddad,
Our country would not be what it is today without people like you. Along with so many other people, I am so grateful for what you have done for this country. I am proud and lucky to have you as a grandad. I have always looked up to you immensely and, even though I don't always show it, I love all your stories that you tell us about the war and what life was like when you were younger.

I love you, Granddad. I hope you had a blast today. You <u>deserve</u> it.

Love,
Jennifer

Dear Granddad,
I'm sure that today was a proud day for you and I hope that you enjoyed it! I also hope that it was an

accurate reflection of your importance to our country. I still remember when I interviewed you for my school report in the 9th grade. I was so proud to get up in front of my class, as your granddaughter, and share your experience of World War II. Your story and the level of bravery and selflessness that you demonstrated is truly remarkable. I look up to you and admire you so much. I love you!

Love,
Christine

Dear Uncle Glenn,
It is not possible for me or any other non-veteran to comprehend what it was like to climb into a cold B-17 knowing that things might not go successfully on the mission ahead. To me, that is ultimate courage.
I think of you and your accomplishments often. I think of the things you went through in that POW camp and I think of the amazing accomplishments of your civilian life and career after the war. You are an inspiring reminder of traditional American virtues: discipline, determination, and can-do attitude. I hope to embody these traits in my own adult life, especially in this complicated and challenging time.
I'm really grateful to have to known you these past few years, and look forward to spending more time together.

With utmost admiration and love,
Steven J. King

Dear Uncle Glenn,

...We hope the monuments and memorials in Washington D.C. do an adequate job of reminding generations to come of the tremendous cost and sacrifice required of the men and women who fought for us in WWII. I know over the years we have thanked you for sharing your stories and experiences, but I don't think we thanked you enough for your service and sacrifice.

With all our hearts we love you and thank you for all that you did during your time in World War II. Your legacy will live on through our teaching of our children and grandchildren ensuring they never forget. We hope you had the trip of a lifetime and that you actually enjoyed flying again.

With all our love,
Greg and Karen (Glenn's nephew and wife)

Dear Glenn,
I wanted to take this opportunity to thank you for all you have done for so many. I am only sixteen and I have no idea what it is like to be away from home and fighting for my country. I have heard that it is hard for people like you to talk about the time you spent fighting for our freedom. My freedom. I just wanted you to know that there are many people who have not forgotten what you have done for all of us...
I am glad that you are able to take this trip and see the war memorials. I hope that in some small way it will remind you of how many people are proud of what you

and other have done. I do not know what I will do or be when I grow up. I know that the actions you took made it possible for me to be able to wait and decide when the time is right for me. Your sacrifices are our gift. Please enjoy your trip and have a long and memorable life.

Adam – Joliet, Illinois (unknown to Glenn)

Glenn still marvels at the number of thank-you letters written to him from people he does not know and will never meet.

A few weeks after Honor Flight, Glenn received a handkerchief with the insignia of the 8th Air Force and his first name embroidered on it from a young woman from Mokena, Illinois. It was her mother's handiwork, she explained in her letter. "We appreciate all the hard work you have done to help our country. I have a lot of respect for you, though I don't even know you. . . ."

Through Honor Flight Chicago, Glenn was invited to share his story at Naperville's Maplebrook Elementary School. It had been awhile since he had addressed a room of junior high students, never mind a gymnasium packed with grade school kids. "I relished the idea of doing it," Glenn says, "but I didn't have my normal confidence in making my speech, so I typed up a summary."

As he began to talk, silence reigned, Glenn says. "There wasn't even the normal rustling and noise." He was impressed by the children's deportment and was deeply honored after his speech when two girls presented him with jars filled with coins that had been collected in support of Honor Flight Chicago.

A uniformed young man serving with the 169th Airlift Squadron stood at the back of the room. He wound his way through the crowd of students to Glenn. He ripped the unit patch off his sleeve and handed it to Glenn. "I want you to have this," he said.

Glenn keeps the patch tucked in his desk, next to his wings.

October 2010: Glenn at the Wall of Freedom in Washington, D.C., during his
visit to the National World War II Memorial hosted by Honor Flight Chicago.

Glenn in 2014 at the age of ninety, with a model of a B-17.
He lives on his own in Naperville, Illinois.

Epilogue

One of the revelations in preparing this book was reading documents online about Glenn's last mission. Documents from the War Department, declassified in the 1970s, are viewable at Fold3.com, where J. Kurt Spence has posted the fruits of his research, starting with the American flyers whose POW mug shots he found at the National Archives. By investigating their stories and sharing the information online, his research led me to B-17 navigator William W. Varnedoe and his book *The Story of Van's Valiants of the 8ᵗʰ Army Air Force: A History of the 385ᵗʰ Bomb Group in World War* II, in which he details the combat missions flown from Great Ashfield.

Incredibly, Varnedoe, normally part of the George H. Crow crew, was flying in the same formation as Glenn on March 2, 1945, as a substitute navigator with Thornton Audrain's crew. In a personal email, he wrote about his third mission: "On Audrain's right wing was Tipton in A/C (aircraft) No. 44-8417. Tipton was on his 3rd mission, his first with his crew. Tipton's crew and Crow's crew had trained together at Avon Park, Florida; both flew over the Atlantic at the same time and were both assigned to the 385th and 550th on the same orders. Crews seldom really knew each other well, but our two crews were a little better acquainted."

Hoping to shed a bit more light on what had happened to the scheduled bombardier on Tipton's crew, I asked Varnedoe if he knew of

Davidow or why he might have missed the briefing. He said he didn't know the man or why he failed to show.

Varnedoe added that he "did not see the Tipton B-17 getting hit and going down, because at that time I was manning the right cheek gun which had jammed! I had to take off my big, clumsy glove, put on a small silk one to keep from touching bare metal at 40 below. I cleared the jam in that gun (a bent link in the ammo chain). So when I looked up from that task, the 17 ahead (piloted by Vaadi) and both of my wing 17s (piloted by Tripp and by Tipton) had disappeared – shot down!!"

This is Varnedoe's emailed account of Mission 261 on Friday, March 2, 1945:

> The 385th dispatched aircraft from three squadrons on this mission. The 550th Bomb Squadron was positioned as the low squadron and given the code nickname "Clambake George Lo."
>
> During the early morning briefing, the crews were told that they would be flying over fighter fields of the Luftwaffe but were not expected to encounter much resistance. The weather that day was bad. The primary target was to be a Ruhland oil refinery, but heavy clouds diverted the group to the secondary target, a railroad marshalling yard at the southern outskirts of Dresden, Germany. The bombing altitude was set at 23,000 feet.
>
> 2nd Lt. Kenneth G. Tipton and his crew of the B-17G serial number 44-8417, were part of the mission. Tipton was on his second mission and his first with his crew who had just recently arrived in England. The lead and high squadron turned slightly short of the IP, but the low squadron saw the mistake and continued on to the correct checkpoint. This left a large gap in front of the low squadron.
>
> The official report stated the low squadron was "straggling" 2 or 3 miles behind the main group. The German Air Force took advantage of this break in the formation

and attacked the low squadron. A group of six Focke-Wulf (Fw 190s) and three Messerschmitt (Me 109s) fired their 20 mm shells and made several passes from the rear and side. Three B-17s in the low squadron were hit. Several other aircraft made emergency landings in France.

At approximately 10:43 (a.m.), the Flying Fortress being piloted by Tipton was hit by fighters over Oschatz, Germany. (Oschatz was the German fighter field as well as the IP.) After the initial attack on the Low Squadron, they also made a pass at the High Squadron. The B-17 piloted by Krahn in the High Squadron (a spare, who took Bloom's place after take-off) was also shot down. Two others B-17s got hit in their gas tanks and had to land at an occupied airfield in France, due to low gas.

In his 2003 edition of *The Story of Van's Valiants,* Varnedoe describes Mission 261 on page ninety-three:

On the bomb run, Tipton's B-17 was knocked out during the first attack. The co-pilot, Ed Craig, recalls that they were hit in the radio room and the tail section, then sustained a burst in the main fuel tank. Nos. 1 and 4 were on fire, the turbos out and the controls were half-shot away. They began a split-S, but the auto pilot held them level enough for all to jump.

The tail gunner, John, was killed on impact with the ground, but all the others were captured and sent to a prisoner camp. On the way to interrogation, Jack, the navigator, was hit in the mouth by a brick thrown by a civilian and had a tooth knocked out.

Craig and Glenn, the bombardier, were captured near Oschatz, then sent to Frankfurt for interrogation before being sent to a POW camp. At the time, no one saw any parachutes and many reported that the plane had exploded. . . . Mission 261 proved the Luftwaffe was not yet quite dead."

The official Air Corps report on the crash simply stated: *Aircraft 44-8417 was hit by enemy aircraft cannon fire, fell back of formation and blew up almost immediatley* (sic). *The wrecked plane fell into the clouds, the tops of which were then at 18,000 ft. No chutes were seen.*

Glenn has read several accounts about his last mission while preparing for this book. Over the years, being computer-averse, he had not sought out the Air Corps' official version of what happened. While he is not completely reconciled with some of the details he has read about the mission, he says the information is "close enough."

The amount of information on the Internet pertaining to Glenn's experiences in the war – films made at the liberation of Moosburg, websites devoted to prisoners of war, the 385th Bombardment Group Association website, even the Missing Air Crew Reports (MACRs) of the U.S. Army Air Forces, 1942-1947 – is staggering. Because Glenn has spent his life looking forward, these revelations of his life as a twenty-year-old bombardier have been both compelling and unsettling.

Glenn only recently learned that members of the 385th Bomb Group have been holding reunions on and off since 1956. He says he assumed any reunion information would have been detailed in his copy of *Air Force Magazine*; unfortunately, that was not the case.

If it's too late to don dancing shoes and attend a gathering of the survivors of the 385th, Glenn has no regrets. It is enough that he has borne witness to his war experiences in classrooms to children mesmerized by his stories. The connections he has made in the community through his service are woven carefully with rich and varied threads. Clearly, his has been no ordinary life.

ACKNOWLEDGEMENTS

All writers are in need of great editors, and so the author wishes to thank Dr. Barbara F. Luebke, professor emerita of journalism, University of Rhode Island, for her keen editorial insight and patience.

Also sincerest thanks to:

J. Kurt Spence, for connecting documents and photos with the stories of downed airmen and sharing the information with the world on Fold3.com; Bill Varnedoe, author of *The Story of Van's Valiants of the 8th Army Air Force: A History of the 385th Bomb Group in World War II*; the 385th Bomb Group Association, whose online presence greatly enhanced my understanding of the war as it was waged from Great Ashfield; Gregory Hatton and his POW research on b24.net, where the march from Nuremburg to Moosburg is described; Bill Wylie of Wylie Design, for his cover design; Jeff Lautenberger for his shot from the nose of the B-17 *Aluminum Overcast*; and Ed Wiles, for his invaluable audio, video and photography assistance.

And, of course, thanks to Glenn for having me over on those many afternoons to hear the stories of your life. It has been my honor.

ABOUT THE AUTHOR

Sue Johnpeter grew up in Bronxville, New York, the daughter of a World War II bombardier instructor and a newspaper reporter who met while dancing in Big Spring, Texas.

She received a Bachelor of Journalism degree from the School of Journalism at the University of Missouri-Columbia, thirty-four years after Glenn King was there.

At one time or another, she has been a newspaper reporter, elementary school computer instructor, internet image editor, blogger, photographer, gencalogist, mother and grandmother.

She lives with her husband, Charlie, in Naperville, Illinois, just down the road from Glenn.

Made in the USA
Monee, IL
27 July 2021

73997374R00095